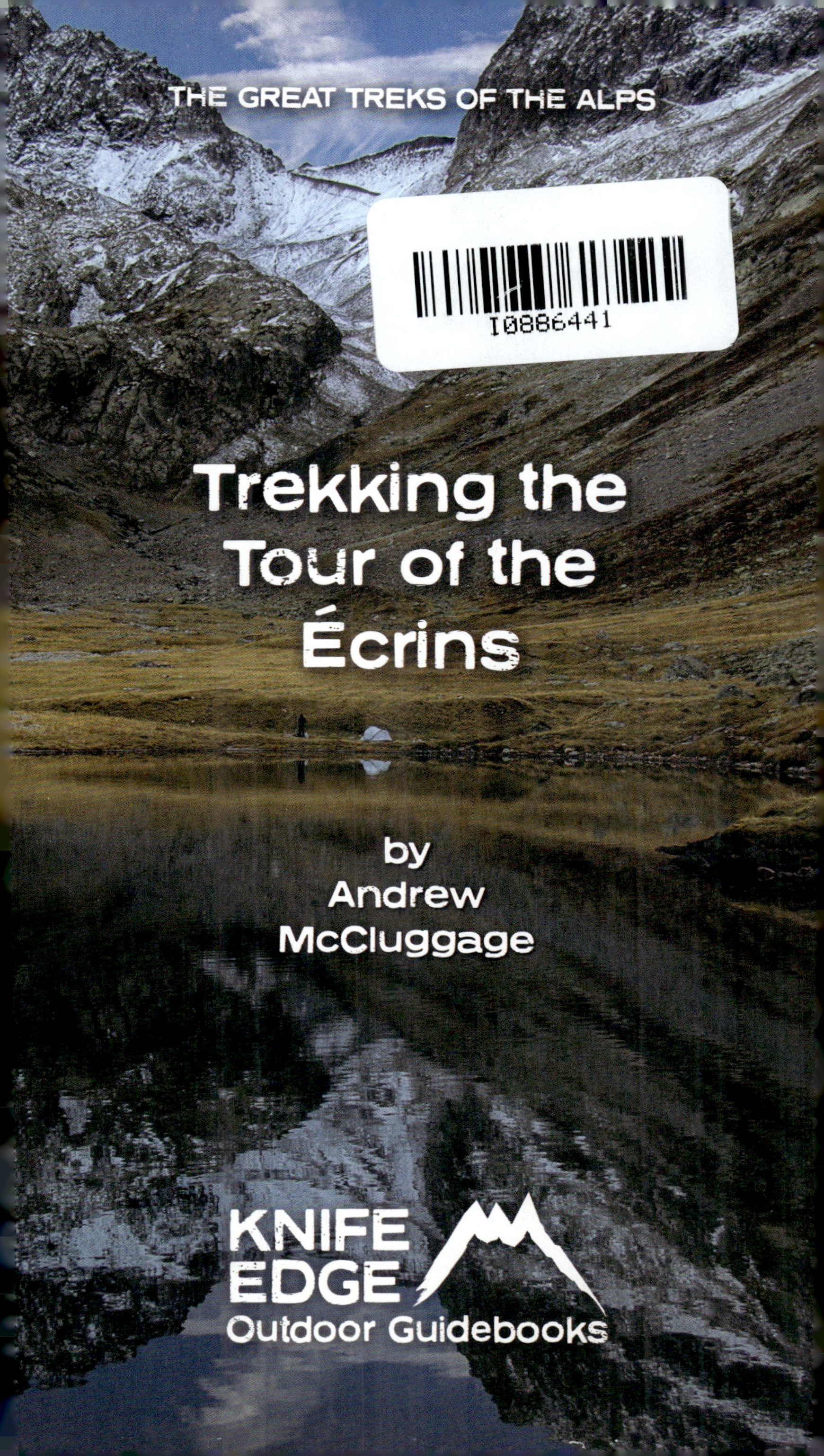

THE GREAT TREKS OF THE ALPS

Trekking the Tour of the Écrins

by
Andrew McCluggage

KNIFE EDGE
Outdoor Guidebooks

About the Author

Andrew McCluggage is an outdoor writer and photographer from Northern Ireland. After 20 years as a corporate lawyer, he decided to do something interesting and started writing walking guidebooks.

His first book was Walking in the Briançonnais, a beautiful part of the French Alps. Since then, he has written a variety of guidebooks for hiking and trekking.

Other Knife Edge Outdoor Guidebooks written by Andrew include:

- **Tour du Mont Blanc**
- **Trekking the Dolomites AV1**
- **Walker's Haute Route: Chamonix to Zermatt**
- **Trekking the Corsica GR20**
- **Trekking the Mallorca GR221**
- **Trekking Iceland's Laugavegur Trail**
- **Trekking the West Highland Way**
- **Trekking the Hadrian's Wall Path**
- **Trekking the Coast to Coast Path**
- **Trekking the Cotswold Way**
- **Trekking the Cleveland Way**
- **Trekking the South Downs Way**
- **Walking Chamonix-Mont Blanc**
- **Walking Brittany**
- **Northern Ireland: the Unmissable Walks**
- **The Mourne Mountains**
- **Big Hikes in the Mourne Mountains**

Admiring the peaks of the Écrins National Park

KNIFE EDGE Outdoor Guidebooks

Publisher: Knife Edge Outdoor Limited (NI648568)
12 Torrent Business Centre, Donaghmore, County Tyrone, BT70 3BF, UK
www.knifeedgeoutdoor.com

Second edition 2024
ISBN: 978-1-912933-60-0

First edition 2019

A catalogue record for this book is available from the British Library.

Front and back covers: Sheep grazing below Col de St-George (Stage 2b)

Title page: Reflections of Col de la Muzelle in Lac de la Muzelle (Stage 8b)

This page: The view from Col de la Muzelle (Stage 8b)

Front cover flap: Lac Noir (Stage 2c)

Back cover flap: Lac Lauvitel (Stage 9a)

All routes described in this book have been recently walked by the author and both the author and publisher have made all reasonable efforts to ensure that all information is as accurate as possible. However, while a printed book remains constant for the life of an edition, things in the countryside often change. Trails are subject to forces outside our control. For example, landslides, tree-falls or other matters can result in damage to paths or route changes; waymarks and signposts may fade or be destroyed by wind, snow or the passage of time; or trails may not be maintained by the relevant authorities. If you notice any discrepancies between the contents of this guide and the facts on the ground, then please let us know. Our contact details are listed at the back of this book.

Contents

The Fournel valley (Stage v5)

Getting Help

Emergency services number: dial 112

Distress signal

The signal that you are in distress is 6 blasts on a whistle spaced over a minute, followed by a minute's silence. Then repeat. The acknowledgment that your signal has been received is 3 blasts of a whistle over a minute followed by a minute's silence. At night, flashes of a torch can also be used in the same sequences. Always carry a torch and whistle.

Signalling to a helicopter from the ground

Help Required

Raise both arms in the shape of a 'Y'

Help Not Required

Raise one arm and extend the other arm down and outwards

WARNING

Hills, cliffs and mountains can be dangerous places and walking is a potentially dangerous activity. Some of the routes described in this guide cross potentially hazardous terrain. You walk entirely at your own risk. It is solely your responsibility to ensure that you and all members of your group have adequate experience, fitness and equipment. Neither the author nor the publisher accepts any responsibility or liability whatsoever for death, injury, loss, damage or inconvenience resulting from use of this book, participation in the activity of mountain walking or otherwise.

Some land may be privately owned so we cannot guarantee that there is a legal right of entry to the land. Occasionally, routes change as a result of land disputes.

The clearly marked ToE on the way to Col de la Vaurze (Stage 7c)

Introduction

The Tour of the Écrins (designated the GR54) is a worthy member of that great trilogy of French Alpine treks which also includes the Tour du Mont Blanc and the Vanoise High Route. It is an incredible long–distance route involving a circuit of the Écrins Massif which is one of the 'crown jewels' of the French Alps. On the way, it passes through some of the best sections of the Parc National des Écrins (Écrins National Park or ENP) which is one of Europe's largest national parks and which was incorporated to protect the pristine natural environment that the trek crosses.

Visually, the Tour of the Écrins (ToE) is one of the finest mountain walks in Europe as it traverses some very unspoilt alpine terrain. The walker also passes through some spectacularly situated villages and hamlets where food and accommodation can be found. But the route stays well away from any large towns so there is a clear sense of wilderness and adventure. Those who walk these trails witness wild and spectacular scenery which is accessible to very few.

The ToE takes between 9 and 12 days and is normally walked clockwise. Notwithstanding statistics published elsewhere, we find the route to be approximately 193km in length with an intimidating 12,000 metres of climbing and descent. 14 magnificent mountain passes (or cols) are crossed. Accordingly, it is not the easiest route but with the right preparation, planning and approach is perfectly manageable. And that is where this guide comes in: most of what you need to know to plan, and prepare for, the ToE is here within these pages and the entire route is described in detail to guide you on the trail itself. Furthermore, unlike some other books, this one contains real maps: for each stage, there are real IGN 1:25,000 scale maps to go with the accurate and concise route descriptions.

We aim to ensure that you have the best chance possible of completing the trek. We place great importance on the correct preparation and we focus in detail on modern lightweight equipment (see 'Equipment'). We also believe that it is crucial to match your itinerary to your experience, fitness and ability. Accordingly, we have included a unique itinerary planner which has 4 different itineraries to choose from. For each itinerary, we have completed for you all the difficult calculations of time, distance and altitude gain/loss. This makes it easy for you to design a manageable itinerary that suits your specific needs. Once on the trail, you will be able to relax and fully enjoy one of the world's great treks.

The Écrins Massif

The Écrins Massif is the highest range of mountains in France outside of the Mont Blanc Massif: a stunning wilderness which is located roughly half-way between Geneva and Nice. It has everything you would expect from an alpine region: snow frosted summits, beautiful valleys and pastures, sparkling azure lakes filled with trout, carpets of wild flowers, the soothing sound of cow bells and a lifetime supply of paths available to walkers. However, the Écrins seems to do things better than in other regions: the sheer scale of this vast range is breathtaking and the lack of visitors (discussed below) gives the terrain a perceptible sheen of wildness and ruggedness not found elsewhere. Rightly, much of the massif is protected by the ENP (see below) and consequently, it has suffered much less development than alpine areas further north.

With so much beauty on offer, you might wonder why the region attracts far fewer visitors than the busy Northern Alps and why so few English speaking hikers have even heard of it? Well the answer is partly practicality: the Écrins Massif is geographically more isolated, being further from motorways and transport hubs such as Geneva. And perhaps as a result, many foreign walkers have preferred to frequent the more easily accessible mountains around Geneva. And in recent decades, tourist infrastructure has not developed at the same pace as in the wealthier Northern Alps so this possibly continues to keep numbers down.

The 'Bucket List Phenomenon' also provides part of the answer. Everyone these days has a imaginary list of 'things to do before you die'. On the list of many will be to walk in the highest range of mountains in Western Europe, in the shadow of the famous and mighty Mont Blanc. Sadly, fewer people consider hiking in the second highest range in the French Alps, in the shadow of (the less well known) Barre des Écrins, the highest mountain in France outside of the Mont Blanc Massif.

Whatever the reason, the lack of visitors is a clear advantage for hikers who will easily find peace and solitude amongst scenery of indescribable beauty. In fact, outside the six weeks of the peak summer season, these wonderful mountains are practically empty. And even during peak times, the Écrins is tranquil compared to better-known regions. In the age of mass tourism such an experience is a rarity in the Alps.

To underline this point, the surface area of the ENP is approximately 50% of surface area of the entire Lake District National Park in England. However published statistics indicate that although the latter welcomes more than 16 million visitors each year, the former apparently only gets around 800,000. This suggests that the Écrins attracts only 10% of the visitors per km^2 that come to the Lake District.

Because the Écrins has experienced relatively little development, it retains a rural feel which has been greatly diluted elsewhere. There are fewer large ski resorts interfering with the natural beauty and absent therefore are the millionaires' chalets that are common in other areas. It is fair to say that the Écrins is still largely a French region for French people.

Another major draw is the climate. Anecdotally, locals are fond of telling you that the region enjoys 300 days of sunshine each year. The veracity of this statement is up for debate but it is true that the climate in the Écrins is generally drier and milder than that of the Northern Alps. This means more sunny walking days, slightly higher temperatures and less rain, than in alpine regions further north. In the hectic modern world when vacation time is so short, favourable sunshine odds cannot be discounted lightly.

In summary, those who do not visit are missing out. Anyone who knows these amazing mountains will tell you that they are as magnificent as any in Europe and more unspoilt. And it is for good reason that aficionados of the region tend to be fiercely loyal to it. Come and you will not regret it: in our opinion, the Écrins should be at the top of your bucket list!

History of the ToE

The ToE was the brainchild of the mountain guide, Roger Canac. In 1962/63 he marked out the route with a few of his friends and sought out places to sleep at the end of each stage. In 1964, the trail was officially named the GR54 but it was not the clearly waymarked path that you see today. At that time, the ENP had not even been created and the route utilised ancient paths, previously used to connect neighbouring towns and valleys. In fact, many cols (such as the Col de l'Aup Martin) had not been crossed for decades so early hikers were pioneers.

Écrins National Park (ENP)

The ENP was created in 1973 to protect the heart of the Écrins Massif after pressure from naturalist groups, mountaineers and CAF. It was the fifth national park in France. It consists of 270,000 hectares of alpine territory between the towns of Grenoble, Briançon and Gap. Its rough boundaries are the rivers Romanche (N), Guisane (N), Durance (E) and Drac (W). The Écrins Massif contains more than 150 peaks exceeding 3000m and more than 10,000 hectares of glaciers. The highest peak is the Barre des Écrins (4102m). There are more than 700km of paths available to hikers.

How hard is the ToE?

The ToE is a multi-day trek with significant distances to travel each day. It crosses remote landscapes of mountains, hills and valleys: you will need to climb and descend significantly, on a daily basis, to negotiate the undulating terrain. Sometimes, the climbs and descents are steep and challenging. As the days go by, such exertions take their toll on your body, both physically and mentally. Accordingly, a reasonable level of fitness is required: the fitter you are at the start of the trek, the better your chances of success and the more you will enjoy it.

Many who have completed the TMB (the most famous Alpine trek) look to the ToE for their next trekking experience. Accordingly, it can be useful to compare these two treks. Although they are normally completed over a similar number of days, the ToE is longer (193km compared to 174km) and has more climbing (12,000m compared to 9,700m). Furthermore, the terrain on the ToE is occasionally more exposed and challenging than that on the TMB. In summary, the ToE is a little harder than the TMB.

Before undertaking a multi-day trek, it is sensible to train in advance: there is no substitute for training hikes, carrying a pack. Although not absolutely necessary, previous experience of backpacking and camping will help.

Direction and start/finish points

Normally the ToE is walked clockwise. It can also be tackled in an anti-clockwise direction but this is slightly more difficult due to the spacing of the accommodation and the steepness of the climbs.

The default approach described in this guide is the traditional clockwise one, with the route starting and finishing at the town of le Bourg d'Oisans to the NW of the range. However, the Route Planner below makes it easy to plan an alternative approach, starting from la Grave, le Monêtier-les-Bains, or Vallouise. When choosing a starting point, bear in mind that Stages 5a and 5b need to be hiked on the same day unless you are equipped to stay in an unmanned refuge. The 5a/5b combination makes for the toughest day on the trek: unless you are already in good shape for walking, or intend to take the bus to Entre-les-Aygues, it makes sense to have a few days to warm up before tackling it.

Starting Point	Pros	Cons
Le Bourg d'Oisans	Easy access by bus **Initial stages easier, allowing warm–up before the harder stages after Vallouise** Best supermarkets and shops **Good bars and restaurants for a victory celebration** Good selection of places to stay	Not much doorstep hiking for spare days at the end **Busy all summer as it is a Mecca for road cyclists, particularly if the Tour de France is passing through in July** Accommodation is harder to find so book earlier
La Grave	A stunningly beautiful place to start and finish **Good shops** Best bars and restaurants **Good selection of places to stay** Plenty of doorstep hiking and mountain biking for spare days at the end	Harder to access **Less warm-up before the harder stages after Vallouise**
Le Monêtier-les-Bains	A pretty town **Good shops** Good bars and restaurants **Good selection of places to stay** Plenty of doorstep hiking and mountain biking for spare days at the end	Harder to access **Only one stage to warm-up before the harder stages after Vallouise**
Vallouise	Perhaps the most beautiful village in the region **Easy access by train and bus/taxi** Supermarket and a few shops **Plenty of doorstep hiking opportunities for spare days at the end** A fabulous place for relaxing after the ToE	No warm up before the harder stages so you will need to be in shape before starting **Fewer bars and restaurants** Fewer places to stay in the town itself

The Onde Valley (Stage 5a)

Guided tours, self-guided tours or independent walking?

A frequently asked question is whether to walk independently or with an organised group. The answer is a personal one and depends upon your own particular circumstances and requirements. For many, the decision to organise the trek themselves, and to walk independently, can be almost life-changing, opening the door for other challenges in the future. There is much satisfaction to be gained from planning and navigating a trek yourself and the sense of achievement on completion is to be savoured.

However, the independent trekker usually carries a full pack and is responsible for all daily decisions such as pacing, which way to go at junctions, when to stock up with food and water, and choice of route in bad weather. For some, this may be too great a burden on top of the physical effort required simply to walk the route. For those walkers, a guided group is a great solution: the tour company typically organises food, accommodation and transfer of luggage most nights. And the guide makes all the decisions, enabling the walker to concentrate on the walking. There are a few tour companies (mainly based in France) which operate guided trips on the ToE, however, they do not always cover the full route so check before booking.

A self-guided tour would be a sensible middle-ground between independent trekking and guided tours but unfortunately, there do not appear to be any tour companies at present which offer these for the ToE: hopefully, this will become possible in the future. On a self-guided tour, the tour company books all the accommodation and provides advice and information on walking the route. However, you walk the trail without a guide. Often, they can transfer your baggage to your accommodation each night so you only need to carry a small day-pack on the trail. Even confident trekkers (who would be perfectly capable of walking independently) can benefit from booking a self-guided trip because it takes away the stress of having to book accommodation in a foreign language.

When to go

The weather window for hiking the ToE is quite short: the trekking season starts towards the end of June and ends around the middle of September. Even in this period, high winds, heavy rain, and low cloud (which reduces visibility), can occur: occasionally, it can even snow on the trail. You will probably hike in fine weather but you should prepare for the worst. Throughout the trekking season, there is plenty of daylight. The relative merits of each season are discussed in detail below but, taking all the factors into consideration, we prefer to hike the ToE in the first two weeks of September.

Late June: this can be the most beautiful time for walking. The weather is sunny and warm and the peaks are frequently at their most photogenic, still fully frosted with snow. Summer haze has not yet arrived so visibility is generally excellent with wide-ranging views. Of course there is still rain at this time of year but this usually lessens as the season progresses. There are carpets of spring wild-flowers and there are fewer visitors so accommodation is easier to find and significantly, the mountains are more peaceful. However, as with all Alpine treks, in some years, high cols can be snow–covered until early July, making parts of the route difficult and/or dangerous: in such conditions, crampons and/or an ice axe might be helpful. There are now some very light, compact crampons available which weigh a mere 300g so carrying them just in case is not the burden it once was.

July and August: this is the main summer season when the high cols are normally passable. As the period progresses, the trails gradually become busier. The busiest time is the four week period commencing around the 14 July, when most of the French take their annual vacations: hut accommodation is harder to find and advance booking is recommended unless you are camping. It can be hot, reaching more than 30°C. Mornings often start with clear and sunny skies and heat up as the sun gains height.

If there is to be cloud or haze, often this will arrive in the afternoon when thunderstorms are more likely. Start walking early in the morning to complete the main climb while the temperature is cooler. From the middle of August, the number of trekkers starts to decrease and it becomes easier to find a bed. As the month progresses further, the days become gradually shorter but there is still plenty of daylight for hiking.

September: this can be the best month for walking as the weather is often more settled than in summer. Skies are usually clear and visibility excellent. Daytime temperatures are still warm but evenings get cooler and the days get shorter. From the last week in August, visitor numbers thin out rapidly so the mountains are quiet and there is less demand for accommodation. However, from mid-September some accommodation starts to close for the season so check availability in advance. If you are properly equipped, you can stay in the winter rooms of refuges after they officially close (see Accommodation).

October: this is a very beautiful time, with autumn colours to rival those in New England. Careful planning is needed to undertake the route at this time of year. As the month progresses, the possibility of snowfall on the cols increases which could make them impassable or dangerous. Check the weather forecasts carefully along the way to avoid getting trapped by snow between cols. If fresh snow is forecast, do not set out. Most accommodation will be closed so you could carry camping gear and/or stay in the winter rooms of the refuges. You will need to be prepared to carry more food as there will be fewer places to stock up. Trekking in October is for experienced and well-equipped hikers only.

Month	Pros	Cons
Late June	Pleasant temperatures **Frequent sunny skies** Good visibility **Wild flower season** Fewer trekkers **Hut beds easier to find** Longest days	Most snow on trail: high cols and peaks occasionally inaccessible due to snow
July/August	Generally reliably fine weather **High cols normally passable** Long days	The hottest period **Sometimes hazy** Afternoon thunderstorms **Visitor numbers highest** Hut beds harder to find **Some snow remains in early July**
September	Pleasant temperatures **Frequent sunny skies** Excellent visibility **Fewer visitors** Hut beds become easier to find **Autumn colours** Still sufficient daylight	Accommodation closes as the month progresses **Shorter days** Cooler evenings **Increasing possibility of snow**
October	Autumn colours **Frequent sunny skies** Excellent visibility **Fewer visitors**	Greater possibility of snow **Much accommodation closed** Short days **Cold mornings and evenings**

Using this book

This book is designed to be used by walkers of differing abilities. Many guidebooks for long-distance treks rigidly divide the route into a fixed number of long day-stages, leaving it up to the hiker to break down those stages to design daily routes which suit his/her abilities. This book, however, has been laid out differently to give the trekker flexibility: it divides the ToE route into 21 shorter stages which you can combine to design daily routes that meet your own specific needs.

Each stage covers the distance between one accommodation option and the subsequent one: all accommodation options on the route are the start/finish point of a stage. You can choose how many of these stages you wish to walk each day. Each stage has its own walk description, route map and elevation profile.

The labelling of the stages uses a combination of numbers and letters. It is a simple system but requires a little bit of explanation. Firstly, we have divided the route into 9 'Sections' (numbered from 1 to 9 starting at le Bourg d'Oisans and moving clockwise): each Section represents one day of our base 9-day schedule. Within each Section, the route has been further broken down into two or three shorter stages: these stages are labelled with a number between 1 and 9 (representing the relevant Section that the stage is part of) and also a letter. So, for example, the first stage in Section 3 is 'Stage 3a', the second stage is '3b' and the third stage is '3c'. Take a look at the detailed Itinerary Planner below and all should become clear.

The Itinerary Planner includes a range of tables outlining 4 suggested itineraries of 9, 10, 11 and 12 days. In each table, the maths have been done for you so there is no need for you to waste time (and mental strength) working out daily distances, timings and altitude gain/loss. The 9 day itinerary is our base itinerary which is suitable for fit walkers who want to complete the route in the shortest time. However, most hikers will want to take more time and use the 10, 11 or 12 day itineraries.

Of course, the suggested itineraries are only suggestions. You can shorten or lengthen your day to suit yourself: just decide how many stages you want to walk that day. It is up to you. As there is accommodation/camping at the end of most stages, it is easy to design your own bespoke itinerary and adjust it on the ground as you go.

For example, day 1 of the standard 9-day itinerary involves walking Stages 1a and 1b. However, you could decide to extend your day by walking Stages 1a, 1b and 2a, all on the same day. Or you might be tired and decide to shorten your day by walking only Stage 1a. With some other guidebooks, you would have to work out how to split stages yourself, involving some complicated maths to plan distances and times going forward. This guide, however, does all the hard mental work for you.

In this book:

Timings indicate the approximate time required by a reasonably fit walker to complete a stage. They do not include stoppage time. Do not get frustrated if your own times do not match ours: everyone walks at different speeds. As you progress through the trek, you will soon learn how your own times compare with those given here and you will adjust your plans accordingly.

Walking distances are given in kilometres (km) to match maps and signposts in France. One mile equates to approximately 1.6km.

Place names in brackets in the route descriptions indicate the direction to be followed on signposts. For example, "('Vallouise')" would mean that you follow a sign for Vallouise.

Ascent/descent numbers are the aggregate of all the altitude gain or loss (measured in feet and metres) on the uphill or downhill sections of a stage. As a rule of thumb, a fit walker climbs 1000 to 1300 feet (300 to 400m) in an hour.

Elevation profiles are provided for each Section, indicating where the climbs and descents fall on the route.

Real maps are provided. These are extracts from 1:25,000 scale maps produced by IGN, the French mapping agency. We believe that these are the best maps available for the ToE. On the maps, we have marked the route of the trek, the start/finish points of stages and significant waypoints. On each map, N is at the top of the page.

The following abbreviations are used:

BCE	Before the Common Era (a secular alternative to 'BC')
CAF	Clubs Alpins Français
CE	The Common Era (a secular alternative to 'AD')
ENP	Écrins National Park or Parc National des Écrins
OR	Off-route
ToE	Tour of the Écrins or GR54
WW2	World War 2
TL	Turn left
TR	Turn right
SH	Straight ahead
N, S, E and W, etc.	North, South, East and West, etc.
N-S	North to South
S-N	South to North

A morning inversion on the descent from Refuge de Vallonpierre (Stage 6b)

Itinerary Planner

Mountain rescue helicopter in the EMP

Stage	Start	Time (hr)	Distance km	Distance miles	Ascent m	Ascent ft	Descent m	Descent ft
1a	le Bourg d'Oisans	2:15	6.5	4.0	752	2467	30	98
1b	le Châtelard	4:35	15.6	9.7	694	2277	780	2559
2a	Clavans-le-Bas	1:00	1.7	1.1	250	820	60	197
2b	Besse-en-Oisans	2:00	4.9	3.0	694	2277	0	0
2c	Plateau d'Emparis	4:00	12.4	7.7	400	1312	1181	3875
3a	la Grave	1:15	3.4	2.1	340	1116	169	554
3b	Villar d'Arêne	1:10	2.8	1.7	85	279	66	217
3c	Pont d'Arsine	5:00	17.6	10.9	680	2231	877	2877
4	le Monêtier-les-Bains	6:30	19.6	12.2	955	3133	1262	4141
5a	Vallouise	3:20	13.1	8.1	820	2690	39	128
5b	Cabane du Jas-Lacroix	5:00	11.9	7.4	830	2723	971	3186
6a	Refuge du Pré de la Chaumette	4:50	10.7	6.7	1190	3904	706	2316
6b	Refuge de Vallonpierre	2:15	6.8	4.2	0	0	872	2861
6c	Refuge du Clot - Xavier Blanc	1:45	7.2	4.5	90	295	393	1289
7a	la Chapelle-en-Valgaudemar	1:00	4.5	2.8	0	0	67	220
7b	Villar Loubière	2:30	5	3.1	952	3124	0	0
7c	Refuge des Souffles	4:30	10.8	6.7	648	2126	1358	4456
8a	le Désert-en-Valjouffrey (to Valsenestre junction)	3:30	9.3	5.8	1050	3445	790	2592
8b	Junction near Valsenestre	3:45	10	6.2	1142	3747	493	1618
9a	Refuge de la Muzelle (to la Danchère junction)	4:30	9.5	5.9	465	1526	1594	5230
9b	Junction near la Danchère	2:30	10.1	6.3	15	49	281	922
Finish	le Bourg d'Oisans							

Suggested Itineraries

9 Days: very fit and experienced walkers. Day 8 is a monster!

Day	Stages	Time (hr)	Distance km	Distance miles	Ascent m	Ascent ft	Descent m	Descent ft
1	1a, 1b	6:50	22.1	13.7	1446	4744	810	2658
2	2a, 2b, 2c	7:00	19.0	11.8	1344	4410	1241	4072
3	3a, 3b, 3c	7:25	23.8	14.8	1105	3626	1112	3648
4	4	6:30	19.6	12.2	955	3133	1262	4141
5	5a, 5b	8:20	25.0	15.5	1650	5414	1010	3314
6	6a, 6b, 6c	8:50	24.7	15.4	1280	4200	1971	6467
7	7a, 7b, 7c	8:00	20.3	12.6	1600	5250	1425	4675
8	8a, 8b	7:15	19.3	12.0	2192	7192	1283	4210
9	9a, 9b	7:00	19.6	12.2	480	1575	1875	6152

10 Days: fit and experienced walkers.

Day	Stages	Time (hr)	Distance km	Distance miles	Ascent m	Ascent ft	Descent m	Descent ft
1	1a, 1b	6:50	22.1	13.7	1446	4744	810	2658
2	2a, 2b, 2c	7:00	19.0	11.8	1344	4410	1241	4072
3	3a, 3b, 3c	7:25	23.8	14.8	1105	3626	1112	3648
4	4	6:30	19.6	12.2	955	3133	1262	4141
5	5a, 5b	8:20	25.0	15.5	1650	5414	1010	3314
6	6a, 6b, 6c	8:50	24.7	15.4	1280	4200	1971	6467
7	7a, 7b, 7c	8:00	20.3	12.6	1600	5250	1425	4675
8	8a	3:30	9.3	5.8	1050	3445	790	2592
9	8b	3:45	10.0	6.2	1142	3747	493	1618
10	9a, 9b	7:00	19.6	12.2	480	1575	1875	6152

Plateau d'Emparis (Stage 2c)

11 Days: perhaps the most common approach.

Day	Stages	Time (hr)	Distance km	Distance miles	Ascent m	Ascent ft	Descent m	Descent ft
1	1a, 1b	6:50	22.1	13.7	1446	4744	810	2658
2	2a, 2b, 2c	7:00	19.0	11.8	1344	4410	1241	4072
3	3a, 3b, 3c	7:25	23.8	14.8	1105	3626	1112	3648
4	4	6:30	19.6	12.2	955	3133	1262	4141
5	5a, 5b	8:20	25.0	15.5	1650	5414	1010	3314
6	6a	4:50	10.7	6.7	1190	3904	706	2316
7	6b, 6c, 7a	5:00	18.5	11.5	90	295	1332	4370
8	7b, 7c	7:00	15.8	9.8	1600	5250	1358	4456
9	8a	3:30	9.3	5.8	1050	3445	790	2592
10	8b	3:45	10.0	6.2	1142	3747	493	1618
11	9a, 9b	7:00	19.6	12.2	480	1575	1875	6152

12 Days: take your time and experience an unmanned refuge.

Day	Stages	Time (hr)	Distance km	Distance miles	Ascent m	Ascent ft	Descent m	Descent ft
1	1a, 1b	6:50	22.1	13.7	1446	4744	810	2658
2	2a, 2b, 2c	7:00	19.0	11.8	1344	4410	1241	4072
3	3a, 3b, 3c	7:25	23.8	14.8	1105	3626	1112	3648
4	4	6:30	19.6	12.2	955	3133	1262	4141
5	5a	3:20	13.1	8.1	820	2690	39	128
6	5b	5:00	11.9	7.4	830	2723	971	3186
7	6a	4:50	10.7	6.7	1190	3904	706	2316
8	6b, 6c, 7a	5:00	18.5	11.5	90	295	1332	4370
9	7b, 7c	7:00	15.8	9.8	1600	5250	1358	4456
10	8a	3:30	9.3	5.8	1050	3445	790	2592
11	8b	3:45	10.0	6.2	1142	3747	493	1618
12	9a, 9b	7:00	19.6	12.2	480	1575	1875	6152

Accommodation

On some stages, there are a variety of places to stay. However, on others there may be only one option: in such circumstances, it is wise to book ahead. Forward booking is also advisable at weekends and during the French summer holidays (the four week period starting around 14 July). In June and September, fewer people walk the route so accommodation is rarely full. However, remember that before mid-June, and from mid-September onwards, some accommodation will be closed. Most accommodation will let you store luggage: as the ToE is a circular route, you can collect your bags again at the end.

Hotels: the majority of hotels will be in the one to three star categories and quality varies. Normally, they offer 'half-board' (bed, breakfast and dinner) which can be good value. Most hotels have their own websites.

Gîtes d'étape: traditionally, a gîte would have been comparable to a youth hostel, offering beds in dormitories and evening meals. These days gîtes are often more upmarket: private rooms are normally available and they can be better than some hotels. Most gîtes now have their own websites.

Chambres d'hôte: comparable to bed and breakfast accommodation in the UK. Quality can vary widely.

Refuges: these are mountain huts which offer dormitory accommodation, meals and alcohol. Refuges are often situated in the heart of the mountains where they are accessible only to the walker: the settings are spectacular. A stay in a refuge can be one of the highlights of a mountain adventure such as the ToE. Although prices have risen in recent years, they are still good value: bed, dinner and breakfast should cost around €50-65. If you are lucky, the gardien (manager) may let you sample some homemade Génépy, a potent liqueur made from a plant only found in the high mountains. Mattresses are provided but you will need a sleeping sheet which is a thin bag made of silk or cotton: they can be purchased cheaply at most outdoor shops in the UK or France. There are usually facilities for charging electronic devices but you may have to queue. Some refuges accept credit cards but others only take cash.

Refuges are normally manned from mid-June to mid-September but outside these times many have a 'salle d'hiver' (winter room) where you can stay. The facilities in the winter rooms vary but usually they will have blankets and a wood-burning stove for heat. You will have to bring your own food and sometimes cooking equipment.

Most of the refuges on the ToE are run by one of the local 'Clubs Alpins Français' (CAF or French Alpine Club). Further information on each CAF refuge, including the facilities available in each salle d'hiver, can be found at the website of the Fédération Française des Clubs Alpins et de Montagne (www.ffcam.fr). Members of CAF and other national mountaineering clubs usually get a discount on the price of a bed.

Campsites: most towns and villages have campsites which are normally clean and well maintained. Wild camping or bivouacking in the ENP is generally permitted between 19:00 and 09:00 but only if you are at least one hour's walk from the ENP's limits and any roads. However, along the shores of Lac de la Muzelle and Lac Lauvitel, camping is only permitted in the specifically authorised zones (indicated on the signs at the lakes): this restriction was introduced in 2023 because higher numbers of people bivouac in these areas. At Lac Lauvitel, you can only camp at les Selles and the nearby beach. At Lac de la Muzelle, you can only camp on the S side of the lake. Outside the ENP, wild camping is usually tolerated provided that you are discreet and only stay for one night. Wherever you pitch up, ensure that you carry out all rubbish and bury any toilet waste well away from watercourses.

Hut etiquette

- On arrival, check in at the warden's office.
- Take off your boots and wet clothing at the front door and store them in the places provided at the entrance.
- Do not make noise after 10pm as most walkers go to bed early.
- If you change your plans, cancel your reservation as soon as possible to allow someone else to take your place.

La Grave in autumn

Walkers cross the glorious Plateau d'Emparis on a typical September day (Stage 2c)

Accommodation Listings

Le Sirac dominates Stage 6a

Symbol	Meaning	Symbol	Meaning
[bed]	Dormitory	[fork & knife]	Evening Meals
[lock & key]	Private Room	[croissant]	Breakfast
[tent]	Camping	[cart]	Food shop
[glass]	Drinks	[wifi]	WiFi
[burger]	Lunch	OR	Off-route
[snowflake]	Winter Room		

Stage	Name	Facilities	Contact Details
1a Le Bourg d'Oisans	Hotel l'Oberland	Private Room, WiFi, Drinks, Breakfast, Lunch, Evening Meals	04 76 80 24 24 www.hoteloberland.com
1a Le Bourg d'Oisans	la Clé des Bois (Chambre d'Hôtes)	Private Room, WiFi, Drinks	06 08 71 61 02/06 08 71 61 02 info@lacledesbois.com www.lacledesbois.com
1a Le Bourg d'Oisans	Hotel des Alpes	Private Room, WiFi, Drinks, Breakfast, Lunch, Evening Meals	04 76 80 00 16 www.hoteldesalpesoisans.com
1a Le Bourg d'Oisans	Hotel Terminus	Private Room, WiFi, Drinks, Breakfast, Lunch, Evening Meals	06 23 34 56 91 Leterminus38@outlook.fr www.leterminusoisans.com
1a Le Bourg d'Oisans	Hotel de Milan	Private Room, WiFi, Drinks, Breakfast, Lunch, Evening Meals	04 76 80 01 23 info@surlaroutedesalpes.com www.surlaroutedesalpes.com
1a Le Bourg d'Oisans	Camping la Piscine	Camping, Private Room, Drinks, Breakfast, Lunch, Evening Meals	04 76 80 02 41 infos@camping-piscine.com www.camping-piscine.com
1a/1b Le Châtelard	Hôtel La Forêt de Maronne	Private Room, WiFi, Drinks, Breakfast, Lunch, Evening Meals	06 37 11 38 95 laforetdemaronne@gmail.com www.laforetdemaronne.com
1b/2a Clavans-le-Bas	Auberge du Savel	Dormitory, Private Room, WiFi, Drinks, Breakfast, Lunch, Evening Meals	07 50 65 55 15/06 72 65 66 16 www.auberge-du-savel.fr

Stage	Name	Facilities	Contact Details
1b/2a Clavans-le-Bas	Chambres d'Hôtes		04 76 80 27 03
2a/2b Besse-en-Oisans	Gîte Le Sarret		04 76 80 06 22 gitelesarret@gmail.com www.gite-le-sarret.com
2a/2b Besse-en-Oisans	Escale en Oisans Chambres d'Hôtes		07 82 92 82 67 contact@escale-en-oisans.com ccroquand.wixsite.com
2b/2c Plateau d'Emparis	Refuge Les Moutèrres		06 67 39 48 07/06 87 15 70 79 refugelesmouterres@orange.fr www.refugelesmouterres.com
2b/2c Plateau d'Emparis	Refuge du Fay		06 81 44 74 40
2c Le Chazelet	Gîte Chez Baptiste		06 75 53 94 24 gite.chezbaptiste@gmail.com www.chezbaptiste.fr
2c Les Terrasses	Restauberge La Reine Meije		06 19 60 62 80 f.jongen@reinemeije.fr www.reinemeije.com
2c/3a La Grave	Gîte Le Rocher		04 76 79 96 46 gite.le.rocher@free.fr www.gite-lerocher.fr
2c/3a La Grave	Auberge Edelweiss		04 76 79 90 93 info@hotel-edelweiss.com www.hotel-edelweiss.com
2c/3a La Grave	Hotel le Serac		04 76 79 91 53 jean-michel@hotel-le-serac.com www.hotel-le-serac.com
2c/3a La Grave	Hotel Castillan		04 76 79 90 04 www.le-castillan.com
2c/3a La Grave	Camping de la Meije		06 08 54 30 84 campingmeije@gmail.com www.camping-delameije.com
3a/3b Villar d'Arêne	Auberge aux Trois Frênes		04 76 79 90 65 info@3frenes.com www.3frenes.com
3a/3b Villar d'Arêne	Hotel les Agneaux		04 76 79 90 62 info@hotel-lesagneaux.com www.hotel-lesagneaux.com
3a/3b Villar d'Arêne	Hôtel Le Faranchin		04 76 79 90 01 contact@lefaranchin.com www.lefaranchin.com
3b/3c Pont d'Arsine	Gîte le Pas de l'Âne		04 76 79 94 28 www.gitelepasdelane.com
3c l'Alpe de Villar d'Arêne	Refuge de l'Alpe de Villar d'Arêne		+33476799466 www.ffcam.fr
3c l'Alpe de Villar d'Arêne	Chalet-Refuge de Chamoissière		09 82 12 46 24 chaletrefugechamoissiere@gmail.com www.chaletrefugedechamoissiere.fr

Stage	Name	Facilities	Contact Details
3c Le Casset	Gîte Le Rebanchon		06 24 37 41 44 contact@lerebanchon.com www.lerebanchon.com
3c/4 Le Monêtier-Les-Bains	Camping Municipal		07 89 56 58 77 camping@monetier.com
3c/4 Le Monêtier-Les-Bains	Gîte Le Flourou		04 92 24 41 13 contact@leflourou.com www.leflourou.com
3c/4 Le Monêtier-Les-Bains	Hotel de l'Europe		04 92 24 40 03 hotel-de-leurope@wanadoo.fr www.hotel-europe-monetier.com
3c/4 Le Monêtier-Les-Bains	Hotel les Colchiques		04 92 24 41 42/06 86 75 10 43 www.hotel-lescolchiques.com
3c/4 Le Monêtier-Les-Bains	Hotel le Monêtier		04 92 55 40 70 contact@lemonetier.com www.lemonetier.com
3c/4 Le Monêtier-Les-Bains	Auberge du Choucas		04 92 24 42 73 choucas@aubergeduchoucas.com www.aubergeduchoucas.com
4 Ailefroide (OR)	Camping d'Ailefroide		06 08 22 82 09 campingailefroide@gmail.com www.ailefroide.fr
4 Ailefroide (OR)	Chalet Hotel Ailefroide		06 77 96 36 55/04 92 23 32 01 contact@chalethotel-ailefroide.com www.chalethotel-ailefroide.com
4 Ailefroide (OR)	Hotel Engilberge		04 92 23 32 05 www.hotel-engilberge.com
4 Le Sarret	La Paille Maison d'Hôtes		07 52 03 87 97 boisterrepaille05@gmail.com www.lapaille05.fr
4 Le Sarret	Gite-hôtel Auberge La Blanche		04 92 23 44 62/06 79 74 19 02 www.gite-lablanche.fr
4/5a Vallouise	Hotel les Vallois		04 92 23 33 10 hotel@lesvallois.com www.hotel-05.fr
4/5a Vallouise	Hotel l'Edelweiss		06 60 90 01 54 hotel.vallouise@gmail.com www.hotel-edelweiss-vallouise.com
4/5a Vallouise	Camping Huttopia Vallouise		04 92 23 30 26 www.europe.huttopia.com
4/5a Vallouise	Gite L'aigliere		06 83 14 12 35/04 92 23 72 64 gite.aigliere.vallouise@gmail.com www.gite-aigliere.com
5a	Camping area at Pont des Places	Free of Charge	Unmanned
5a/5b	Cabane du Jas-Lacroix	Free of Charge	Unmanned

Stage	Name	Facilities	Contact Details
v5 Col de la Pousterle	Refuge de la Pousterle	Open on request	04 92 23 14 55/06 70 51 13 01 Closed at the date of press: may reopen in the future
5b/6a	Refuge du Pré de la Chaumette		04 92 55 95 34 www.ffcam.fr
6a/6b	Refuge de Vallonpierre		04 92 55 27 81 refugevallonpierre@gmail.com www.vallonpierre.com
6b/6c	Refuge du Clot - Xavier Blanc		09 88 77 38 62/06 67 41 24 21 www.ffcam.fr
6c/7a La Chapelle-en-Valgaudemar	Camping Les Marines		06 14 38 43 33 contact@campinglesmarines comwww.campinglesmarines.com
6c/7a La Chapelle-en-Valgaudemar	Camping Larches & Gite Communale Les Mélèzes		04 92 55 23 01
6c/7a La Chapelle-en-Valgaudemar	Hotel du Mont Olan		04 92 55 23 03 hotel@mont-olan.fr www.mont-olan.fr
7a/7b Villar Loubière	Camping Municipal des Eaux Douces		06 45 29 60 63 campingdeseauxdouces@gmail.com campingdeseauxdouc.wixsite.com
7b/7c	Refuge des Souffles		04 92 55 22 91 www.ffcam.fr
7c/8a Le Désert-en-Valjouffrey	Gîte les Arias		06 18 27 70 28 At date of press, ownership had just changed: contacts details are likely to change
7c/8a Le Désert-en-Valjouffrey	Auberge de l'Eterlou		04 76 30 25 12 www.aubergeeterlou.com
7c/8a Le Désert-en-Valjouffrey (OR)	Camping les Faures		04 56 56 21 84/07 69 14 23 78 ladorefaures@gmail.com www.campingdesfaures.fr
8a/8b Valsenestre (OR)	Gîte le Béranger		09 74 74 73 84 giteleberanger@gmail.com www.giteleberanger.com
8b/9a	Refuge de la Muzelle		04 76 79 02 01/09 72 63 87 37 www.refugedelamuzelle.fr
9a/9b La Danchère	Lauvitel Lodge		04 76 80 06 77 info@lelauvitel.com www.lelauvitel.com
9a/9b La Danchère (OR)	Hotel au Bon Accueil		04 76 80 06 72 info@hotelaubonaccueil.com www.hotelaubonaccueil.com
9b Le Vert	Gîte Marmotte de la Meije		04 76 80 03 62/06 62 52 40 58 valdelameije@orange.fr www.marmottedelameije.fr

Facilities

Stage	Place	Private Rooms	Dormitory Beds	Campsite	Meals/ Drinks (non-residents)	Grocery Shop	Transport
1a/9b	Le Bourg d'Oisans	✓		✓	✓	✓	✓
1a/1b	Le Châtelard	✓			✓		
1b	Combe Haute				✓		
1b/2a	Clavans-le-Bas	✓	✓		✓		
2a/2b	Besse-en-Oisans	✓	✓		✓	✓	
2b/2c	Plateau d'Emparis		✓		✓		
2c	Le Chazelet	✓	✓		✓	✓	
2c	Les Terrasses	✓			✓		
2c/3a	La Grave	✓	✓	✓	✓	✓	✓
3a/3b	Villar d'Arêne	✓			✓	✓	✓
3b/3c	Pont d'Arsine	✓			✓		
3c	l'Alpe de Villar d'Arêne		✓		✓		
3c	Le Casset	✓			✓		
3c/4	Le Monêtier-les-Bains	✓	✓	✓	✓	✓	✓
4/v4	Chambran				✓		

Stage	Place	Private Rooms	Dormitory Beds	Campsite	Meals/ Drinks (non-residents)	Grocery Shop	Transport
4	Ailefroide (OR)	✓		✓	✓	✓	✓
4	Le Sarret	✓	✓		✓		✓
4/v4	Vallouise	✓		✓	✓	✓	✓
5a	Pont des Places			✓			
5a/5b	Cabane du Jas-Lacroix		✓				
5b/6a	Refuge du Pré de la Chaumette		✓		✓		
6a/6b	Refuge de Vallonpierre		✓		✓		
6b/6c	Refuge du Clot - Xavier Blanc		✓		✓		
6c/7a	La Chapelle-en-Valgaudemar	✓	✓	✓	✓	✓	✓
7a/7b	Villar Loubière			✓			✓
7b/7c	Refuge des Souffles		✓		✓		
7c/8a	Le Désert-en-Valjouffrey	✓	✓	✓ (OR)	✓		✓
8a/8b	Valsenestre (OR)		✓	✓	✓		
8b/9a	Refuge de la Muzelle		✓		✓		
9a/9b	La Danchère	✓			✓		
9b	Le Vert	✓	✓		✓		

Food

Lac Lérié is found just off route on Stage 2c

Most accommodation can provide breakfast and dinner. As is usual in France, evening meals are generally excellent: often hearty three course affairs suitable for weary hikers. A starter, often soup or pâté, is normally followed by a main course of meat with vegetables, rice, pasta or salad. This will often be rounded off with dessert or cheese. Vegetarian and vegans options will normally be available on request. Breakfast varies in quality: in refuges which are off the beaten track, it is often the functional minimum of coffee, bread and jam, perhaps with some cheeses or cold meats if you are lucky. Closer to civilisation, quality tends to improve.

Local specialities are often rich and filling: such as Tourtons, nicknamed 'Coussins du petit Jésus' (Cushions of baby Jesus). These are tasty little pastry squares stuffed with fillings such as potato, cheese or meat. Fondues and tartiflette (a tasty concoction of potatoes, cream, ham and Reblochon cheese) are also popular with hungry walkers.

For lunch, there are sometimes restaurants on the route but normally, it is more convenient to picnic amongst the mountains. Fortunately, excellent bread is nothing short of a way of life in France: most towns and villages will have a boulangerie (bakery). And supermarkets and local shops stock a wide range of fantastic cheeses and cold meats. However, a little forward planning is required as there are some stages where there are no shops: stock up in advance or buy ready-made sandwiches at your accommodation. Be particularly organised on the second half of the ToE: there are no shops between Vallouise and la Chapelle-en-Valgaudemar (stages 5a, 5b, 6a, 6b and 6c) or between la Chapelle-en-Valgaudemar and le Bourg d'Oisans (stages 7a, 7b, 7c, 8a, 8b and 9).

How much food do I need?

According to the National Health Service (NHS) in the UK, the recommended daily calorie intake is 2,000 calories for women and 2,500 for men. As you will be expending a lot of energy, it seems sensible to increase this slightly: perhaps a minimum of 2,500 for women and 3,000 for men. Of course, every person has a different metabolism and will have different requirements but this is a good starting point. Also bear in mind that your daily requirement will depend on how far you are planning to hike each day: the further you hike, the more energy you will use and the more food you will need. Remember also to bring a little extra food (over and above your estimated daily requirements) for emergencies.

Suggested daily menu for campers

Breakfast: instant porridge is a good option because it is light and packed with calories. You can get a variety of different flavours. It is also cheap and, in many countries, it is available in supermarkets. You prepare it simply by adding hot water. You can also buy pre-packed freeze-dried breakfast meals: although they are convenient, they are more expensive.

Lunch & snacks during the day: nuts are hard to beat as they are light and packed with energy. Peanuts, for example, have more calories per gram than most other foods. Dried fruit is also good and will help keep your bodily functions regular. Energy bars and candy can help to provide some variety.

Dinner: freeze-dried meals are a good choice. Although they can be expensive, the good quality brands make dinner on the trail something to look forward to. Dried pasta and rice are OK too: you can eat these with packet sauces (prepared by adding water).

Col de Gouiran (Stage 6a)

High above the cloud line in the Vallée de la Haute Séveraisse (Stage 6b)

Travel

Air travel to France: the closest airports in France (with flights in the summer) are Lyon, Marseilles and Nice. Paris Charles de Gaulle is also a good option as trains run directly from the airport to various destinations in France. Turin and Milan in Italy are also close but there is little public transport in the summer between Italy and the Écrins.

Generally, public transport to the Écrins can be slow so, if you are in a group of two or more, hiring a car at the airport can be quicker and cheaper than the group's combined train/bus fares. The ToE is circular so you could leave a car at any of the starting points and pick it up again at the end. All the major rental companies operate at the airports and cheap rates can be obtained via a generic booking website (such as **www.auto-europe.co.uk**). If you are flying into Italy (Turin or Milan) and propose to rent a car, check that your hire car company allows you to cross into France: often there is an extra charge for this. Driving times from the airports to le Bourg d'Oisans are as follows: Lyon (1:45); Geneva (2:30), Turin (3:00), Marseilles (3:30), Milan (4:30), Nice (5:00) and Paris (6:45).

Airport	Public Transport from Airport
Lyon	Train or bus from airport to Grenoble. Then bus to le Bourg d'Oisans, la Grave or le Monêtier-les-Bains.
Turin	Rental car only.
Milan	Rental car only.
Geneva	Train from airport to Grenoble. Then bus to le Bourg d'Oisans, la Grave or le Monêtier-les-Bains.
Marseilles	Train and bus from airport or Marseilles city centre (Marseilles Saint Charles) to l'Argentière-la-Bessée. Then bus or taxi to Vallouise.
Nice	Train from Nice Saint Augustin (15min walk from airport), or Nice city centre, to l'Argentière-la-Bessée. Then bus or taxi to Vallouise. Or bus from airport to Aix-en-Provence or Gap: then train to l'Argentière-la-Bessée.
Paris	Train to Grenoble. Then bus to le Bourg d'Oisans, la Grave or le Monêtier-les-Bains. For further information, see above.

Barre des Écrins (4102m), the highest peak in the massif

Trains: the best train stations for the ToE are l'Argentière-la-Bessée (near Vallouise) and Grenoble. Most ToE trekkers travel to the city of Grenoble because its rail connections to other parts of France (and the rest of Europe) are faster and more frequent than the slow, irregular regional trains that serve l'Argentière-la-Bessée. Grenoble is accessible by train from Paris Gare de Lyon (as well as Paris Charles de Gaulle airport). There are also overnight trains between Paris Austerlitz/Bercy and l'Argentière-la-Bessée: you can book a flat bed and the trains arrive into l'Argentière-la-Bessée early in the morning, allowing you to start the ToE the same day. Any of these train services could be linked with the Eurostar from London or a flight to Paris. For train timetables and tickets, see **www.sncf-connect.com**.

By car: You can take a car to France by ferry from a number of different ports in Ireland or the UK. Alternatively, take a car on the train from the UK through the channel tunnel (**www.eurotunnel.com**). The drive from the French ports to le Bourg-d'Oisans should take 8–9hr. From Calais or Dunkirk, the road to Reims can be preferable to avoid the busy Paris ring road.

Travel to/from the trail-heads

There are four primary trail-heads: le Bourg d'Oisans, la Grave, le Monêtier-les-Bains and Vallouise. Most trekkers start from le Bourg d'Oisans, travelling there by bus from Grenoble: the train station in Grenoble is beside the Gare Routière (where buses depart from).

Primary trail-head	Bus from nearest train station	Duration
Le Bourg d'Oisans	Zou Bus 55 from Grenoble's Gare Routière (**www.zou.maregionsud.fr**)	1.25hr from Grenoble
La Grave	Zou Bus 55 from Grenoble's Gare Routière	1.75hr from Grenoble
Le Monêtier-les-Bains	Zou Bus 55 from Grenoble's Gare Routière	2.5hr from Grenoble
Vallouise	Zou Bus 543 from l'Argentière-la-Bessée	15min from l'Argentière-la-Bessée

On the Trail

Approaching Col de la Valette (Stage 6a)

Costs & budgeting

Long-distance walking in France is relatively inexpensive: no permits are required to hike and, on the trek, there is little to spend your money on. Accommodation tends to be cheaper in the Écrins than in the more popular Northern Alps: in refuges and gîtes, breakfast, dinner and a bed normally costs around €50-65. Hotels costs a bit more: perhaps €60–90 for a room. If you camp and/or cook for yourself, then you could get by on €20–30 each day, or even less if you camp wild.

Weather

The French Alps have a relatively dry and predictable climate compared to mountains in the UK or the US west coast. However, conditions can still change quickly so be prepared for rain. And snow is always possible on cols and summits, even in the middle of summer. Mountains can be dangerous so treat them with respect and caution, even if the weather forecast is favourable.

The region has a number of micro-climates with the weather often differing from valley to valley. It is possible therefore to find blazing sunshine on one side of a col and cloud or rain over the other side. The climate in the W of the range tends to be slightly wetter than the E.

Meteo France, the French meteorological office, provides national, regional and local forecasts at **www.meteofrance.com**. It also has an excellent smart phone app which provides regularly updated local forecasts. Local forecasts are also displayed at tourist information offices and refuges. Or ask the hut gardiens (managers) whose local knowledge of weather (and indeed other matters) is often invaluable: you should follow their advice if they tell you it is not safe to hike.

Paths and waymarking

Normally, paths and tracks on the ToE are well-defined. The terrain undulates regularly and some sections are very steep and/or exposed: sometimes the drops are sheer and occasionally, ropes/chains have been fixed to the rocks for safety. Most paths are well maintained and straightforward to walk upon but there are rocky, challenging sections too. Some paths can be muddy and slippery after rain.

Generally, the route is well marked and navigation is usually straightforward in good conditions: waymarks (red and white) and signs have been strategically placed to assist. However, occasionally, there are sections where paths are less easy to follow and navigation is more difficult: for example, where the trail crosses rocky zones. Because much of the route runs within ENP boundaries, waymarks tend to be placed sparingly to avoid sullying the natural environment with man–made marks: they are found only where absolutely necessary to prevent deviation from the route. A red and white cross on a rock or a tree indicates that you are off the ToE route. Yellow signposts often display time and/or distance to a specific destination: the timings are not always reliable.

In the route descriptions, we do not highlight every junction because the waymarking is so good: generally, we only mention junctions if they are particularly significant or if there are no waymarks. As a rule of thumb, remain on the main path unless instructed otherwise by signs/waymarks on the ground or the maps/route descriptions in this book: however, keep your wits about you because there will of course be the occasional exception to this rule! Also, bear in mind that waymarking is at the mercy of the environment: for example, signs and waymarks are sometimes blown down or destroyed by snow.

On the high points of the ToE, snow can remain into July, covering paths and making progress/route-finding more difficult: follow waymarks carefully because they can be hard to spot against the snow. Snow cover is greatest in June and decreases throughout the summer. After the season begins, the trail will become quickly tracked by others ahead of you but always be wary of following someone else's footprints: there is a good chance that they are on the correct path but it is obviously possible that they may have strayed from the trail. Also, remember that any fresh snow can obscure paths.

If you see mountain biking signs, usually indicated by the letters 'VTT' (Vélo Tout Terrain), then take care: mountain bikes are fast and often quiet and a collision between a walker and a mountain bike could be serious.

ToE waymark

Off Route

Turn left

Typical yellow sign

Maps

In this book, each stage has its own map produced from the official 1:25,000 scale maps made by IGN, the French mapping agency. Although it is possible to compete the route just using these maps, a sheet map can be invaluable, particularly in bad weather. Also, with a sheet map you get a much better feel for the geography of the region as it helps you to identify peaks and landmarks sighted along the way. The best map currently available is Éditions Didier Richard's pocket-sized *GR54 Tour de l'Oisans et des Écrins* (1:50,000). At the date of press, the older Rando Éditions' *A6 Écrins* (1:50,000) and Libris' *Écrins* 1:60.000 were out of print.

Alternatively, check out IGN's Géoportail smart phone app which displays IGN's 1:25,000 maps for the whole of France as well as your location on the maps. Although use of this app is free of charge, you will only be able to download maps when you have access to data on a cell-phone network: there is network along most of the route these days but not everywhere. If you wish to download IGN maps for use offline, then you will need to subscribe to a paid app: IGNRando, for example, costs around €17 for a 1 year subscription.

Storing bags

If you wish to spend some time elsewhere after the trek, then you will probably have additional baggage which you need to store while trekking. The ToE is a circular route so you will return to your starting point at the end of the trek. Normally, a hotel that you have stayed at before starting the trek will store your bags until your return: some may charge extra for this so check when booking.

Baggage transfer

Although the villages and mountain huts of the ToE are remote, most can be accessed by road or 4x4 tracks: this makes it possible for heavy bags to be transported by vehicle each day between overnight stops so that you would only need to carry a small, light day-pack on the trail. Some of the companies offering guided tours on the ToE offer baggage transfers as part of the package. However, not every location can be serviced and accordingly, you will probably need to carry basic gear yourself for a couple of the overnight stays at the more remote refuges such as Refuge du Pré de la Chaumette and Refuge des Souffles. Nevertheless, most days you would be spared from the burden of having to carry a heavy backpack, enabling you to pack more clean clothes and some luxuries. At the date of press, we could not find a business which offered baggage transfer services without the requirement to book a guided tour: hopefully this will change in the future.

For any baggage transfer service, always use a waterproof pack-liner inside the bag to make sure your gear stays dry.

Fuel for camping stoves

Airlines will not permit the transport of fuel so you will need to source it upon arrival, before setting out on the trek. Supermarkets, grocery stores, outdoor shops and campsites in the Écrins usually stock fuel: standard screw-in gas canisters and Campingaz canisters (pierceable and twist-on) are widely available. Along the trail, you should find them in le Bourg d'Oisans, la Grave, le Monêtier-les-Bains, Vallouise and la Chapelle-en-Valgaudemar.

If you need petrol/diesel for a multi-fuel stove, there are service stations along the ToE at le Bourg d'Oisans, la Grave and le Monêtier-les-Bains.

Outdoor shops

There are outdoor shops in le Bourg d'Oisans, la Grave, Villar d'Arêne, le Monêtier-les-Bains and Vallouise.

Drinking water

Drinking water should be one of your primary considerations each day. The sun in the Alps is extremely strong: dehydration and sunstroke are possibilities and you will need more water than usual (perhaps three to four litres per day). Tap water in France is drinkable and you should fill up your bottles each morning before you depart: it is good practice to start the day with at least two litres. Along the trail, you can fill up at the fountains, bars and shops in villages/towns or from the many streams and rivers: plan carefully so that you know where the next water point is and always check your water levels when you pass a water point.

Remember that the volume of water in streams may vary depending upon the season and the amount of rainfall over previous weeks and months: at the start of the season (June), the rivers are usually in full flow but by the end of the season (September), many of the smaller ones may be dry. Although some do it, we do not recommend drinking water from a river, stream or lake, without first dealing with possible contaminants including visible particulates, bacteria, viruses, protozoa (for example, giardia) and parasites.

It is possible to deal with most contaminants using one or more of the methods described below but you should research thoroughly the specific product you are planning to use to understand its effectiveness and any possible risks:

- **Boiling** is the traditional method. A rolling boil of 1min should kill everything in the water. However, it does not remove visible particulates so the boiled water will remain the same colour as when you found it, which can be off-putting. It also uses up a lot of fuel and takes time so is impractical.
- **Filtering** usually removes visible particulates, working miracles by turning coloured water clear. It also normally removes around 99.9% of bacteria, protozoa and parasites. Filters are often cheap and light. It is the quickest method of treatment so it is useful for long-distance routes. However, most filters cannot remove viruses (although these are unlikely to be an issue on the ToE): if you are concerned about viruses then you will need to invest in one of the more expensive filters that remove them or combine filtering with another method (boiling, UV or chemical treatment).
- **Chemical treatment** can remove bacteria, protozoa, viruses and parasites (each product is different so read the labels carefully). However, there are many disadvantages to chemicals: they do not remove visible particulates so the water will remain the same colour as when you found it; water treated with chemicals often has a taste (although you can usually buy different chemicals to deal with that); the water usually cannot be drunk immediately as chemicals take time to kill pathogens; and from a health perspective, consuming chemicals may not be good for you.
- **UV treatment** kills bacteria, protozoa, viruses and parasites. However, it does not remove visible particulates so the water will remain the same colour as when you found it: coloured water can be off-putting and the UV treatment is less effective if the water is not completely clear. That said, coloured water is not usually a problem on the ToE. The most common products are Steripens which are very light.

Perhaps the most practical single method for the ToE is filtering: because virus contamination is unlikely, many hikers drink water which has only been filtered with a standard filter, running a small risk of virus contamination. However, if you prefer to be more cautious, you could combine filtration with UV treatment (using a Steripen): this removes or kills practically everything.

The actual effectiveness of individual products varies and is beyond the scope of this book so do your research beforehand. However, it is worth noting that many products claim to be 99.9% effective indicating that drinking water from wild sources can never be said to be 100% risk free. You will have to weigh up the risks and make up your own mind. You drink the water at your own risk!

	Visible Particulates	Bacteria	Virus	Protozoa	Parasites
Boiling	✗	✓	✓	✓	✓
Filter	✓	✓	Only top of the range filters remove viruses	✓	✓
Chemical Treatment	✗	✓	✓	✓	✓
UV Treatment (such as Steripen)	✗	✓	✓	✓	✓

If, like many, you do decide to drink from natural sources then, as well as treating the water, there are a few rules that you should follow to reduce further any risk:

- Avoid water where there is evidence nearby of animals, especially cows or sheep: carcasses (of dead animals) or faeces can cause contamination
- Do not collect water downstream from buildings or grazing areas
- Preferably drink from moving water. The faster the better
- The bigger the river/stream the better
- Generally the higher the altitude the better

Ticks

As is often the case in Europe, ticks are present in the Alps. They can carry Lyme disease or tick-borne encephalitis so check yourself regularly. Remove ticks with a tick removal tool (making sure that you get all of it out) and then disinfect the area.

Escape Routes

The ToE has many exit points with road access, enabling a walker to leave the route early, but the availability of public transport at these locations may vary (see Facilities above). There are, however, some stages where escape would be difficult and once you start you are committed for a few days. For example, after commencing Stage 5a, you enter remote sections of the ENP and escape would be difficult before the end of Stage 6c.

Pastous

A Pastou keeps watch high up in the ENP

The Écrins is a rural area and sheep are grazed in the high mountains in summer. Often, the shepherd will live at high altitude in a tiny cabin throughout the grazing season. To protect the sheep from wolves (which are now prevalent again) and lynx, a flock usually has a dog to accompany it. Normally the dog is a Pastou (or Patou) which is very large, white and long-haired and is related to an old Pyrenean breed. They are usually raised with the flock so form a close bond with the sheep. Often they growl or bark if you approach the flock. Although uncommon, occasionally visitors to the French Alps are bitten by a Pastou which thought that there was a threat to its sheep. Accordingly, the best advice is to give them a wide berth and assume that there may be a Pastou with any flock. Remember that from afar, the colour and texture of Pastous' coats makes them hard to spot amongst the sheep. In particular, take care when passing flocks of sheep on Stages 5b and 6a.

Equipment

The spectacular Lac de l'Eychauda seen from the Col des Grangettes (Stage v4)

The trekker has no influence over challenges like weather and terrain but can control the contents of a pack carried on the trail. Unless you are on a guided tour which provides a baggage transfer service (see 'Baggage transfer'), you will have to carry all your own gear and many trekkers set off carrying equipment which is unnecessary or simply too heavy. The more your pack weighs, the harder the trek will be: lugging a heavy pack can lead to exhaustion, injury and/or abandonment. If you are intending to carry your own gear, then you should give equipment choice careful consideration: it will be crucial to your enjoyment of the trek and the likelihood of success.

Of course, it is easy to understand why a pack should be light, however, it is much more difficult to put this into practice when there are so many things you 'need' in daily life. With experience, it becomes easier to sift between essentials and luxuries but, if you have not been on a multi-day trek before, this can be an unfathomable dilemma. However, if you follow the advice here and limit yourself to the items on our checklist then you should not go far wrong.

A trekker's base weight is the weight of his/her pack, excluding food and water. If you are not carrying camping gear and cooking equipment, it is perfectly possible to get by with a base weight of 5-6kg (13lb) or less. If you intend to carry camping equipment then, by investing in some modern lightweight gear, you could start the trek with a base weight of 8-9kg (17lb) or less. Many people are quick to tell you that the lighter the gear, the greater the price but that is not always the case. While it is true that lightweight gear can be expensive, there are also some excellent lightweight products which are great value. Tents, sleeping bags and backpacks are the three heaviest items that you will carry so they offer the biggest opportunities for weight-saving. But do not ignore the smaller items either as the weight can quickly add up. Accordingly, if you can afford it, it is sensible to invest some money in gear before you leave home. The lighter your gear, the more you will enjoy the trek and the better your chance of success. Be ruthless as every ounce counts.

Recommended basic kit

When undertaking any long-distance route, you should be properly equipped for the worst terrain and the worst weather conditions which you could encounter. In the Alps, this means that you should carry clothing to combat cold, heat, sun, and rain. Becoming cold and wet in the mountains is unpleasant and can be dangerous. Furthermore, if you are lucky and the sun does shine, you will not want to get sunburn (which can put an end to your trek). Also remember that, even in summer, you could experience snow at altitude.

Layering of clothing is the key to managing body temperature. In cool weather, layers can be added: warm air becomes trapped between the layers, acting as insulation. In warmer weather, you simply remove layers and carry them in your pack. Merino wool or man-made materials are preferable: they are lightweight and warm and they wick moisture away from the skin. Do not wear cotton: it is heavy and it does not dry quickly (making you cold). Always carry a spare set of clothes in case you get wet.

Boots/Shoes	Good quality, properly fitting and worn in. Robust soles (such as Vibram) are advisable. Some use trail-running shoes but many prefer boots with ankle support. Shoes/boots with a waterproof membrane (such as Gore-Tex) are good, particularly if there is snow on the ground.	
Socks	2 pairs of good quality, quick-drying walking socks.	
Camp shoes	It is nice to have shoes to wear in the evenings. Flip-flops or Crocs are a common choice as they are light. However, if you have comfortable hiking boots/shoes then you might consider not bringing camp shoes to save weight.	
Waterproof jacket and trousers	They should be waterproof and breathable.	
Base layers	2 T-shirts and underpants of man-made fabrics or merino wool, which wick moisture away from your body.	
Fleeces	2 fleeces. Man-made fabrics.	
Trousers/shorts	1 pair of lightweight walking trousers and 1 pair of shorts. Alternatively, some prefer 2 pairs of trousers. Convertible trousers are practical as you can remove the legs on warm days.	
Gloves	Lightweight gloves are usually sufficient. However, it is sensible to choose waterproof ones.	
Warm hat & buff	Even in summer it can be cold at altitude, particularly on windy days.	
Down jacket	Even in summer, prepare for low temperatures, especially in the evening and early morning.	
Sunglasses, sun hat, sunscreen and lip salve	The sun in the Alps is strong: do not set out without these items.	
Sleeping sheet	A thin bag made of silk or cotton. Required to sleep in refuges.	
Head-light with spare batteries	A flashlight is useful (in both huts and tents) if you need to go to the bathroom in the night. Furthermore, it is good practice to carry one for emergencies: it can assist if you get caught out late and enable you to signal to rescuers.	

Backpack	Your backpack is one of the heaviest items that you will carry. The difference in the weights of various packs can be surprisingly large. 35-40 litres should be sufficient if you are not carrying camping gear. 45-60 litres should be adequate for campers. If you need a pack bigger than these then you are most likely carrying too much. Look for well-padded shoulder straps and waist band. Much of the weight of the pack should sit on your hips rather than your shoulders.
Waterproof pack-liner	Most backpacks are not very waterproof. An internal liner will keep your gear dry if it rains. Many trekkers use external pack covers but we do not find them to be very useful: they flap in the wind and, in heavy rain, water still leaks into the pack around the straps (so you need an internal liner anyway).
Basic first-aid kit	Including plasters, a bandage, antiseptic wipes and painkillers. Blister plasters, moleskin padding or tape (such as Leukotape) can be useful to prevent or combat blisters. A tick removal tool or card is also recommended.
Map, compass & GPS device	For maps, see p31. A GPS unit or a smart-phone mapping app is a useful addition but they are no substitute for a map and compass: after all, batteries can run out and electronics can fail.
Walking poles	These transfer weight from your legs onto your arms, keeping you fresher. They also save your knees (particularly on descents) and can reduce the likelihood of falling or twisting an ankle. Poles are invaluable in snowy conditions.
Phone and charging cable	A smartphone is a very useful tool on a trek. It can be used for emergencies. Furthermore, apps for weather, mapping and hotel booking are invaluable. It can also serve as your camera, saving weight.
Ziplock plastic bag	A lightweight way of keeping money and passports dry.
Ear plugs	Useful if staying in huts: you will thank us if someone snores!
Emergency food	Carry some emergency food over and above your planned daily rations. Energy bars, nuts and dried fruit are all good.
Toilet paper and trowel	Bring a backpacking trowel in case nature calls on the trail: bury toilet waste and carry out used toilet paper.
Whistle	For emergencies. Many rucksacks have one incorporated into the sternum strap.
Knife	Such as a Swiss Army knife.
Portable battery pack	Although refuges have charging points for electronic devices, they will be in high demand. Accordingly, many people carry their own battery packs: Anker make good ones.
Toiletries	If you wish to take showers at campsites and refuges, a small hotel-size bottle of shower gel should be enough to last the trek, saving weight. An almost empty toothpaste tube will also save weight. Leave that make-up behind!
Towel	A lightweight trekking towel is a good idea if you wish to take showers at campsites or refuges.

Additional gear for campers

Tent: this is one of the heaviest things that you will carry so it provides a big opportunity for weight saving. Some 2-person tents weigh more than 3kg while others weigh less than 0.6kg. The heaviest ones are normally built for extreme winter conditions and are overkill for the normal ToE trekking season. Some of the lightest ones, however, are not particularly robust and the thin material can be prone to damage on rocky ground.

Although a few premium brands charge a lot for their products and there are some very expensive tents at the lightest end of the scale, these days there are plenty of mid-weight tents available at reasonable prices. Tents weighing 1 to 1.6kg often strike a good balance between price, longevity and weight. Consider money spent here as an investment in your well-being and enjoyment of one of the world's great trails. Believe us when we say that a few kgs can be the difference between success and failure.

Your tent should be waterproof to ensure that you stay dry during rainy nights. A footprint is a good idea to protect its base: 'footprint' is a trendy, modern word for what used to be known as a groundsheet. Sometimes you can buy footprints specific to your tent model but we prefer to use a sheet of Tyvek which can be cut to size: Tyvek is extremely tough and is cheaper, and normally lighter, than most branded footprints.

Tent pegs: tent weights provided by manufacturers normally exclude the weight of the pegs. The pegs actually provided with tents tend to be quite heavy and many trekkers buy replacement ones which are lighter. Six heavy pegs can weigh as much as 240g while 6 light pegs can weigh as little as 6g. There are many different types available these days and it is important to match the peg with the type of ground they will be used in. You will usually find grassy pitches on the ToE, and therefore pegs do not need to be overly strong: titanium ones (which are very light) are a good choice although they can be expensive.

Sleeping bag: every sleeping bag has a 'comfort rating': this is the lowest temperature at which the standard woman should enjoy a comfortable night's sleep. There is also a 'lower comfort limit' which is for men. That may sound simple but it is not. Although all reputable sleeping bag manufacturers use the same independent standard, the bags are not tested in the same place so there is a lack of consistency amongst ratings. Also, the ratings are designed with an average man and woman in mind, however, every person is different: some people get colder than others and need a warmer bag. The ratings should therefore be used as a guide only and it is wise to choose a bag with a comfort rating which is at least 5°C lower than the night temperatures that you are likely to encounter.

Between the start of July and the middle of August, a bag with a comfort rating between -5°C and 5°C (depending on whether you sleep hot or cold) is normally sufficient to cope with the likely night temperatures. Outside of this period, it can be prudent to go with something a little warmer in case the weather throws a cold spell at you: perhaps a bag with a comfort rating between -10°C and 0°C. It is quite a difficult decision because although you want to be warm at night, you do not want to bring a bag that is much too warm as that would add unnecessary weight to your pack.

Unfortunately, with sleeping bags, price tends to be inversely proportional to weight. This is largely because the lightest bags are filled with goose/duck down which is expensive. Synthetic bags are also available but they are much heavier so down is a better choice for trekking. The disadvantage of down bags is that they can lose their warmth if they get wet but that is less likely if you have a good tent and pack liner. Our advice is first to decide what comfort rating you will require. Then choose the lightest bag (with that rating) which you can afford.

Sleeping mat: this makes it comfortable for you to sleep on the hard ground and insulates you from the ground's cold surface. There are three types: air, self-inflating and closed-cell foam. The advantages and disadvantages of each are set out below. All factors considered, we prefer air mats although the very lightest ones may not be sufficiently warm for some trekkers. Thermarest's NeoAir Xlite and NeoAir Xtherm are good choices.

Sleeping mat type	Pros	Cons
Air mats: need to be blown up	Lightest **Very comfortable** Most compact when packed **Thicker: good for side sleepers**	Most expensive **Hard work to inflate** Can be punctured **Less warm than self-inflating**
Self-inflating mats: a combination of air and closed-cell foam. The mat partially inflates itself when the valve is opened	Warmest **Very comfortable** Quite compact **More durable than air mats** Firmness is adjustable by adding air	Heavier **More expensive than closed-cell foam** Can be punctured
Closed-cell foam mats	Light **Least expensive** Most durable **Cannot be punctured**	Not compact: needs to be strapped to the outside of your pack **Least warm** Least comfortable

Pillow: some use rolled-up clothing but we prefer inflatable trekking pillows which only weigh around 50g.

Stove: you should choose a stove that uses a type of fuel which is readily available in France. Airlines do not permit you to carry fuel on planes so, if you are flying to France, you will need to source fuel on arrival. Although white gas/Coleman fuel is sometimes stocked in outdoor shops, these days gas is more widely available (see 'On the Trail'). Most gas stoves are designed to fit generic screw-on canisters which are readily available in France. Canisters for Campinggaz stoves (which are popular in France) are widely available too. Multi-fuel stoves that burn petrol and/or diesel are useful but they tend to be heavier, dirtier and more complicated than many gas stoves: the locations of service stations are listed on p32.

Hundreds of different stoves are available, some more complicated than others. Often the lightest ones are the most simple and often the most simple ones are relatively inexpensive. If, like most campers, you will eat dried food such as pasta and rice then your stove will need to do little more than boil water. A basic stove which mounts on top of a gas canister will therefore be adequate: such a stove should also be cheap and lightweight (less than 100g).

Pots: if, like most campers, you will eat dried food such as pasta and rice then you will only need one pot which will do little more than boil water. To save weight, go for the smallest pot that you can get away with. For example, if you are travelling solo and planning to use freeze-dried backpacking meals then you would need nothing bigger than a 500-600ml pot. Titanium pots are usually the lightest but they are slightly more expensive. Get the lightest one that you can afford.

Fork/Spoon: we love Sporks! They have a spoon at one end and a fork at the other. They weigh only 9g and cost very little.

Sheep grazing below Col de St-George (Stage 2b)

Safety

Col de Gouiran seen from Col de la Vallette (Stage 6a)

On a calm summer's day the Alps are paradise. But a sudden weather shift or an injury can alter your circumstances dramatically so treat the mountains with respect and be conscious of your experience levels and physical capabilities. The following is a non-exhaustive list of recommendations:

- The fitter you are at the start of your trip, the more you will enjoy the hiking.
- Start early to avoid ascending during the hottest part of the day and to allow more surplus time in case something goes wrong.
- Do not stray from the waymarked paths so as to avoid getting lost and to help prevent erosion of the landscape.
- Before you set out each day, study the route and make plans based upon the abilities of the weakest member of your party.
- Obtain a weather forecast (daily if possible) and reassess your plans in light of it. Avoid exposed routes if the weather is uncertain.
- Never be too proud to turn back if you find the going too tough or if the weather deteriorates.
- Bring a map and compass and know how to use them. GPS devices are useful too.
- It can be sensible to call ahead to your accommodation and tell them what time you will arrive. If you do not turn up then they can raise the alarm.
- Carry surplus food and clothing for emergencies.
- Avoid exposed high ground in a thunderstorm. If you get caught out in one then drop your walking poles and stay away from trees, overhanging rocks, metal structures and caves. Generally accepted advice is to squat on your pack and keep as low as possible.
- In snowy conditions, follow waymarks carefully and do not leave the route. Be wary of following someone else's footprints: there is always a chance that they have strayed from the trail.
- In the event of an accident, move an injured person into a safe place and administer any necessary first-aid. Keep the victim warm. If possible, use your cell-phone to call for help: the emergency number is 112. If you have no signal then send someone to the nearest hut for help.
- Mountain biking is now very popular in the Alps so watch out. A collision with a bike would not be pleasant.
- Hunting is permitted outside the ENP from September onwards. During this period, it is sensible to wear something brightly coloured.
- When cooking on a camping stove, place the stove on the ground. Avoid using it on a picnic table. We have witnessed a trekker knocking over his stove and spilling boiling water on his legs: this is a sure-fire way to end your trek.

General Information

Plateau d'Emparis (Stage 2c)

Language: French is the first language but many locals will have at least some basic English.

Charging electronic devices: Northern European 2-pin plugs are used so visitors from outside Northern Europe will need an adapter. Refuges have charging points for electronic devices but you may have to queue: many trekkers bring their own portable battery packs.

Money: France uses the Euro(€). On the route, there are ATMs in Bourg d'Oisans, la Grave, le Monêtier-les-Bains and Vallouise. However, it is wise to carry surplus cash in case an ATM is out of order. Credit cards are accepted widely in villages although many refuges accept cash only.

Visas: citizens of the UK, EU, EEC, Australia, New Zealand, Canada or the US do not need a visa for short tourist trips to France.

Cell-phones: these days, there is cell network along most of the trail (particularly in towns and villages). However, in some remote valleys, network coverage is poor. When network is available, it is likely to be a 4G/5G service, enabling access to the internet from smart-phones.

International dialling codes: the country code for France is +33 and the first 0 in the French area code is omitted if calling from outside of France.

WiFi: most hotels and gîtes have WiFi but refuges do not.

Emergencies and rescue: rescue services in France are normally free but this may not always cover helicopter evacuation. Accordingly, it is wise to take out your own rescue insurance. The emergency number is 112.

Medical insurance: depending upon your nationality, any required medical treatment in France may not be provided free of charge so it is wise to purchase travel insurance which covers hiking.

Tourist information: the following websites are useful:

- **www.grand-tour-ecrins.fr:** website for long distance hiking in the **Écrins**
- **www.paysdesecrins.com:** the official tourism website for the **Écrins**
- **www.ecrins-parcnational.fr:** the official website for the **ENP**
- **www.lagrave-lameije.com:** the official tourism website for the village of **la Grave**
- **www.bourgdoisans.com:** the official tourism website for the village of **le Bourg d'Oisans**

Wildlife

Ibex in the ENP

The extremely varied ecosystems mean that there are more than 350 species of vertebrates in the Écrins Massif. Generally, early morning is the best time for sightings. Often the first party on the trail may see many Chamois or Bouquetin but following groups will not see any.

Bouquetin (or Ibex): A member of the goat family with long scimitar shaped horns. It was saved from extinction by the Savoy kings who banned most hunting in 1821 and created a royal reserve in 1856 (which finally became Italy's Gran Paradiso National Park). After a series of reintroductions in the 20th century, they are now fairly widespread throughout the French Alps. In 1989, 16 Bouquetin were introduced into the Valbonnais sector of the ENP from the Vanoise and Vercors parks. In 1995, a further 31 animals were introduced into the Champsaur sector. A GPS tracking program monitors the now well established population.

Chamois: Another type of mountain goat which is smaller than the Bouquetin and is widespread in the Écrins Massif. It has shorter horns which do not have deep ridges. Chamois are frequently spotted in herds. They are much more wary of humans than Bouquetins.

Deer: Various species are common below the tree line. Chevreuil (Roe Deer) are reddish or grey-brown and Daim (Fallow Deer) tend to be brown with white spots. Look out for them when climbing through forests early in the morning.

Marmot

Marmots: Everyone loves these fat rodents which are easily spotted in summer when they graze relentlessly to put on layers of fat to last the long winter hibernation. They live in colonies in grassy parts of the mountains, often standing upright on their hind legs like a meerkat. They whistle as you approach to warn their colony of an intruder.

Sanglier (Wild Boar): A member of the pig family with small tusks. They are common in forests. In the unlikely event that you spot one, keep your distance because they can be dangerous.

Wolves: Hunted to extinction in France in the 1930s. In recent decades conservation efforts in Italy increased their numbers and many have now crossed the border into France through the mountains. They are protected but their presence is controversial and particularly unpopular with shepherds who lose many sheep to them. They are occasionally spotted by walkers.

Other mammals: Squirrels, foxes, badgers and mice are fairly common below the tree line.

Golden eagle

Fish: species of trout are found in most rivers, streams and lakes. Many high alpine lakes also contain Arctic Char.

Lagopède (or Ptarmigan): A grouse-like bird. Its plumage is white in the winter and largely brown in the summer.

Golden Eagle: (pictured left) nearly 40 pairs of these fabulous birds inhabit the Écrins and sightings are common. During the hot parts of the day they can be seen circling in the thermals to gain altitude as they scan the ground for prey.

Gypaète Barbu (or Bearded Vulture): A vulture with a wingspan of up to 3m. In Germany it was given the name 'Lammergeier' ('lamb-hawk') because it was believed that it attacked lambs. Although rare, you are more likely to spot one in the Écrins than further north.

Larch forest W of Chaumette (Stage v6a)

Plants and Flowers

The beautiful and rare Chardon Bleu (Stage v5)

The ENP is home to more than 2,500 plant species including the incredible wild-flowers. June is a fabulous month for flowers, which wait patiently throughout the winter for the snow to clear and then rapidly spring to life. At this time, carpets of different colours cover the slopes and pastures. Although spring is the peak time for flowers, there are still plenty throughout the summer. Watch out for the following:

Alpenrose: a bright pink member of the Rhododendron family which coats the slopes at altitude in June/July.

Viola: a small flower in a variety of colours including yellow, white and blue (or a combination of those colours). It is often found in grassy areas.

Chardon Bleu: a rare blue flower of particular and ephemeral beauty which flowers in summer. The biggest concentration of this plant in Europe can be found in the Fournel Valley on Stage v5. Also look out for them in the flowerbeds of Valsenestre.

Edelweiss: it is the most famous alpine plant, perhaps because it has a song named after it. This rare white flower is striking and hard to spot because it only grows at high altitude (1800–3300m). Look out for it on the Plateau d'Emparis.

Alpenrose

Edelweiss

Joubarbe des Toits

Épilobe des Moraines

Aster des Alpes

Doronic

Route Highlights

Stage	Start	Summary
1a	Le Bourg d'Oisans	A gentle introduction to the ToE with a climb to the peaceful hamlet of le Châtelard.
1b	Le Châtelard	A stroll through two lovely hamlets is followed by a short descent into the forest of the Gorge de Sarenne. Then there is a long (but rarely steep) climb to the Col de Sarenne where there are incredible views of la Meije (3983m) and its glaciers. A steep descent into the Vallée du Ferrand leads to the wonderful hamlet of Clavans-le-Bas.
2a	Clavans-le-Bas	Descend to an old mill and then climb to the immaculately preserved mountain village of Besse-en-Oisans with its historic stone buildings.
2b	Besse-en-Oisans	A steep climb to one of the most scenic places in all the Alps: the bucolic Plateau d'Emparis with its grandstand views of la Meije and its glaciers. This is true 'Sound of Music' territory!
2c	Plateau d'Emparis	A glorious traverse across the grazing slopes of the plateau is followed by a steep descent to the stunningly situated hamlet of le Chazelet. The route continues descending all the way to the town of la Grave with its magnificent setting in front of la Meije.
3a	La Grave	An easy walk (despite one short climb) alongside the River Romanche to the spectacular village of Villar d'Arêne. There are superb views of la Meije on the way.
3b	Villar d'Arêne	Another short stage alongside the crystal clear waters of the River Romanche.
3c	Pont d'Arsine	Climb through the upper reaches of the Romanche Valley to Col d'Arsine, high up in the ENP below the famous Montagne des Agneaux. Descend past the stunning turquoise Lac de la Douche to the village of le Casset with its fascinating museum in an old mill. Then a stroll along the River Guisane brings you to the historic spa town of le Monêtier-les-Bains.
4	Le Monêtier-les-Bains	Climb through lovely larch forest to Col de l'Eychauda. Then descend through the beautiful pastures of the Eychauda Valley. Soon enter the Vallouise Valley with its wonderful views of Mont Pelvoux, one of the highest peaks in the ENP. A short river walk then brings you to the unforgettable village of Vallouise.
5a	Vallouise	Start with a long gentle climb alongside the River Onde to Entre-les-Aygues. From there, head into the Selle Valley with its fabulous cascades and clear blue rock pools. Arrive at the remote unmanned Cabane de Jas Lacroix where you can spend the night if you are properly equipped.

Stage	Start	Summary
5b	Cabane du Jas-Lacroix	There is a difficult but stunning climb to Col de l'Aup Martin. Then a traverse to another col, Pas de la Cavale, where the reward is superb views into both the Fournel and Champoléon Valleys. There follows a relentless knee-jerking drop to the beautiful Refuge du Pré de la Chaumette.
6a	Refuge du Pré de la Chaumette	This remote stage (entirely within the ENP) is a highlight of the ToE. The peak of le Sirac (3441m) dominates the first half of the stage. Climb and cross three spectacular mountain passes in quick succession, Col de la Vallette, Col de Gouiran and Col de Vallonpierre. Then descend to the beautifully situated and modern Refuge de Vallonpierre.
6b	Refuge de Vallonpierre	A long, magnificent descent into the Séveraisse Valley finishes at the pretty Refuge du Clot-Xavier Blanc.
6c	Refuge du Clot-Xavier Blanc	A gentle stroll alongside the River Séveraisse, passing the historical hamlets of le Rif du Sap and le Bourg. Finish at the pretty village of la Chapelle-en-Valgaudemar.
7a	La Chapelle-en-Valgaudemar	Another gentle walk alongside the River Séveraisse brings you to the village of Villar Loubière with its fabulously preserved old mill.
7b	Villar Loubière	A magnificent climb to Refuge des Souffles which has incredible views of Pic des Souffles (3098m), Cime d'Orgières (3061m), Pic Turbat (3028m) and the famous peak of l'Olan (3564m).
7c	Refuge des Souffles	Another highlight of the ToE. A lengthy traverse through incredible alpine scenery is followed by the long (but rarely steep) climb to Col de la Vaurze with its far-reaching views. It is one of the best places from which to view the spectacular l'Olan. Golden eagles are often spotted in this area. A long knee-jerking descent follows, all the way to the remote hamlet of le Désert-en-Valjouffrey.
8a	Le Désert-en-Valjouffrey	After a long climb to Col de Côte Belle (with its beautiful views of the Valjouffrey and Béranger valleys), descend to the immaculately preserved Valsenestre, perhaps the finest hamlet in the region.
8b	Junction near Valsenestre	Begin with another long climb, the last part of which is very steep and quite unstable in places. After crossing Col de la Muzelle, descend to Refuge de la Muzelle which is beautifully set in a mountain cirque overlooking Lac de la Muzelle.
9a	Refuge de la Muzelle	A short climb to the stunning Col du Vallon where there are superlative vistas of la Meije (3983m) and le Râteau (3809m). Then there is a long and relentless descent to Lac Lauvitel and its lovely reflections. After another tiring descent alongside the Lauvitel stream, rest weary legs at the hamlet of la Danchère.
9b	La Danchère	Descend through forest to the village of les Gauchoirs. Then a long flat valley walk leads you past the hamlet of le Vert and into le Bourg d'Oisans where a stiff drink awaits.

The wonderful Refuge de Vallonpierre (Stages 6a and v6a)

Route Descriptions

1a Le Bourg d'Oisans to le Châtelard

le Châtelard

A gentle introduction to the ToE with a climb to the peaceful hamlet of le Châtelard. The start of the ToE was recently the subject of some controversy. The original route, shown on older maps, passed through Campsite la Cascade but after a dispute with the campsite owner a deviation is in place. The route described here is the one in operation at the time of writing.

Chapel in the hamlet of le Rosay (Stage 1b)

Time (hr:min)	2:15
Distance (km)	6.5
Ascent (m)	752
Descent (m)	30
Maximum altitude (m)	1448
Refreshments	le Châtelard
Accommodation	le Châtelard

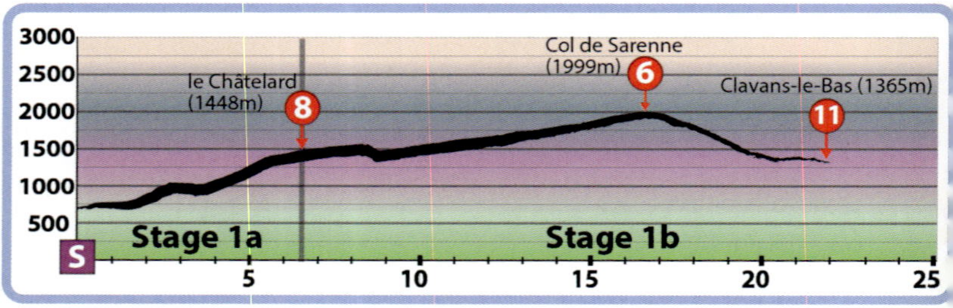

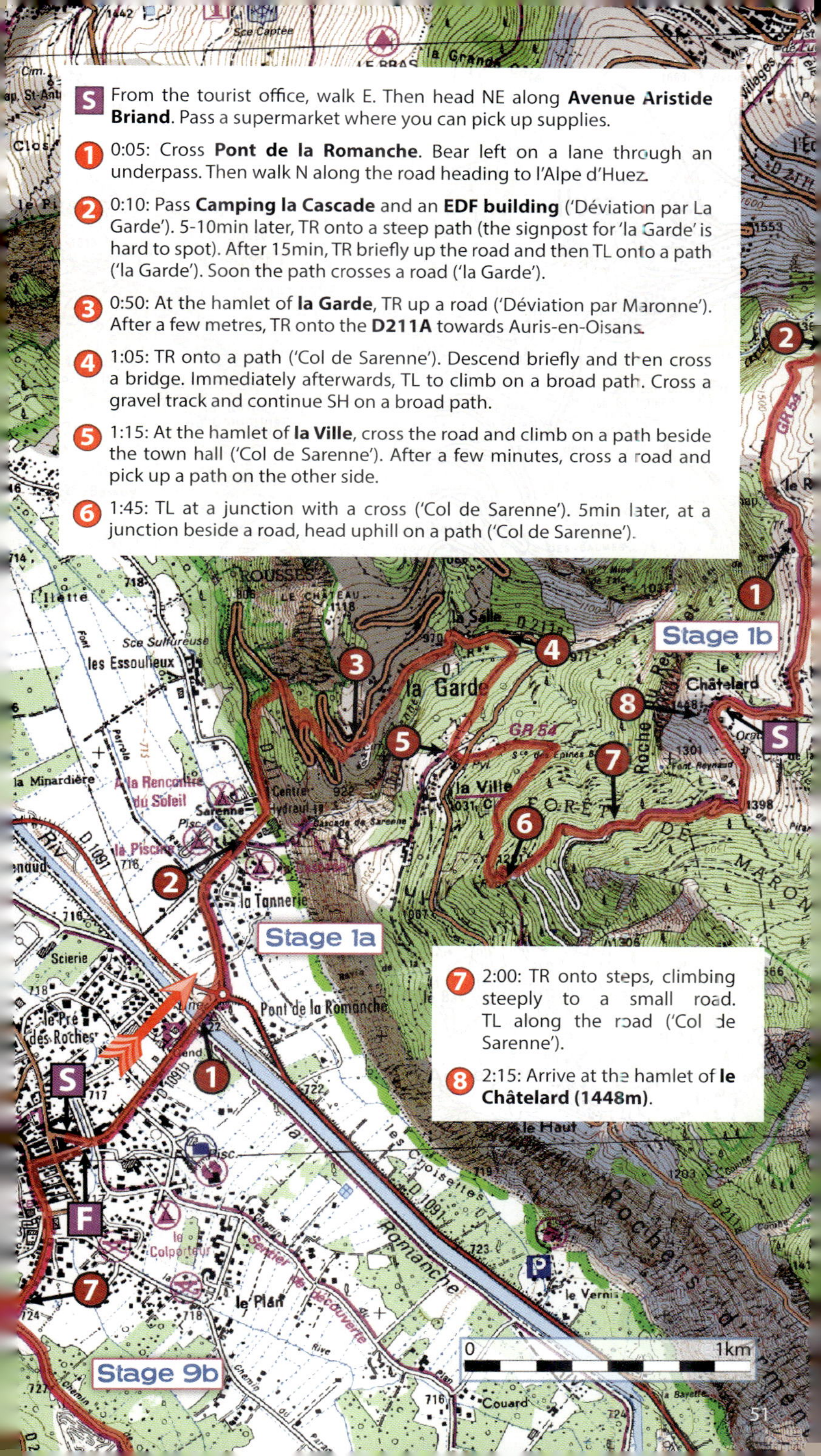

S From the tourist office, walk E. Then head NE along **Avenue Aristide Briand**. Pass a supermarket where you can pick up supplies.

1 0:05: Cross **Pont de la Romanche**. Bear left on a lane through an underpass. Then walk N along the road heading to l'Alpe d'Huez.

2 0:10: Pass **Camping la Cascade** and an **EDF building** ('Déviation par La Garde'). 5-10min later, TR onto a steep path (the signpost for 'la Garde' is hard to spot). After 15min, TR briefly up the road and then TL onto a path ('la Garde'). Soon the path crosses a road ('la Garde').

3 0:50: At the hamlet of **la Garde**, TR up a road ('Déviation par Maronne'). After a few metres, TR onto the **D211A** towards Auris-en-Oisans.

4 1:05: TR onto a path ('Col de Sarenne'). Descend briefly and then cross a bridge. Immediately afterwards, TL to climb on a broad path. Cross a gravel track and continue SH on a broad path.

5 1:15: At the hamlet of **la Ville**, cross the road and climb on a path beside the town hall ('Col de Sarenne'). After a few minutes, cross a road and pick up a path on the other side.

6 1:45: TL at a junction with a cross ('Col de Sarenne'). 5min later, at a junction beside a road, head uphill on a path ('Col de Sarenne').

7 2:00: TR onto steps, climbing steeply to a small road. TL along the road ('Col de Sarenne').

8 2:15: Arrive at the hamlet of **le Châtelard (1448m)**.

1b le Châtelard to Clavans-le-Bas

A stroll through two lovely hamlets is followed by a short descent into the forest of the Gorge de Sarenne. Then there is a long (but rarely steep) climb to Col de Sarenne where there are incredible views of la Meije (3983m) and its glaciers. Sadly, the beautiful old refuge at the col burnt down some years ago. It is not clear whether a new one is to be built. From the col, a steep descent into Vallée du Ferrand leads to the lovely hamlet of Clavans-le-Bas.

Time (hr:min)	4:35
Distance (km)	15.6
Ascent (m)	694
Descent (m)	780
Maximum altitude (m)	1999
Refreshments	None
Accommodation	Clavans-le-Bas

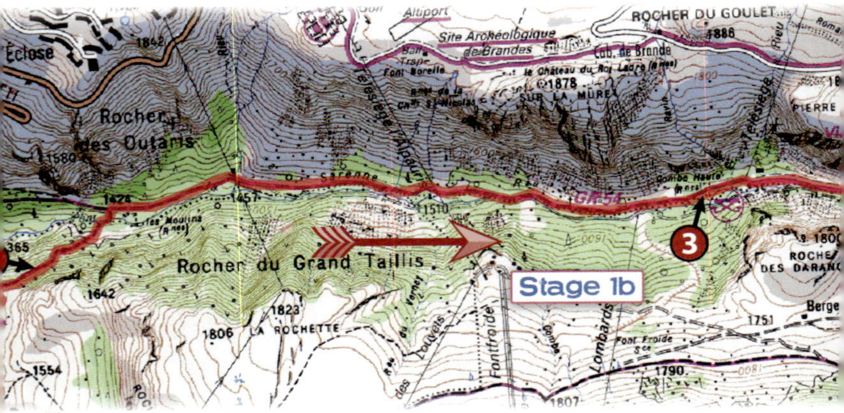

View of la Meije from Col de Sarenne

S Continue on the road through the hamlet of **Maronne**.

1 0:15: TL onto **Chemin de la Chapelle** into the hamlet of **le Rosay**. Take a small path to the right of the chapel. Soon TL at a junction ('Col de Sarenne'). The path undulates for a while, descending into the **Sarenne Gorge**.

2 0:50: Cross a magnificent old bridge and keep SH to a junction. TR ('Col de Sarenne') and pass the remains of an old mill. When the path becomes a track continue E on it, ignoring offshoots. TL at a fork ('Auberge de la Combe Haute').

3 1:30: In front of **Auberge de la Combe Haute**, TL at a fork.

4 2:05: TL onto another track and continue climbing.

5 2:20: TR onto a road. Just afterwards, where the road bends to the right, leave it and head across grass towards a signpost to the S. Before the signpost, TL on a grassy track heading E. When the track meets the road, TL and walk up it.

6 2:45: Arrive at **Col de Sarenne (1999m)**. Just to the right is an amazing viewpoint. Keep SH on the road.

7 3:05: TR onto a path heading steeply downhill ('Clavans'). 10min later, TL in front of a rock (cairns): it is easy to miss this turn. 20min later, at a junction without waymarks, TL and continue downhill towards a track. Cross the track and descend on a faint path. Now there is a confusing array of paths: keep straight downhill following cairns.

8 3:50: Cross a road and descend on a path.

9 4:00: Keep SH descending on a road through **Clavans-le-Haut (1396m)**.

10 4:10: TR and climb on another road. After a few minutes keep SH on a grassy track ('Cimetière des Hugenots'). Shortly after **Cimetière des Hugenots**, TL onto a path. 5min later, TL at a fork.

11 4:35: TR onto a road and enter **Clavans-le-Bas (1365m)**.

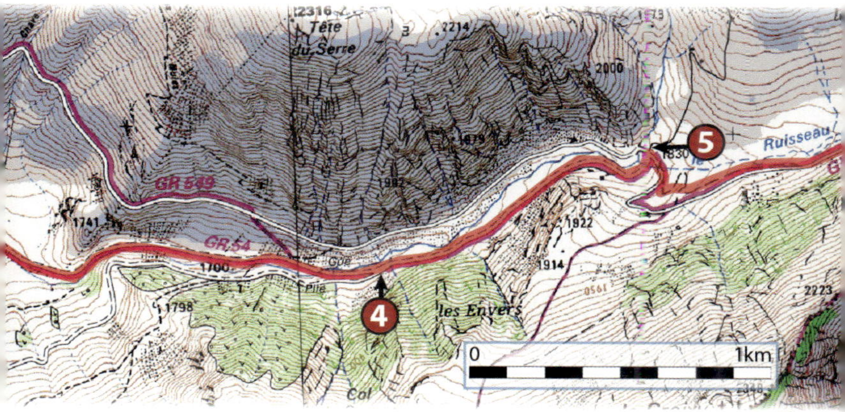

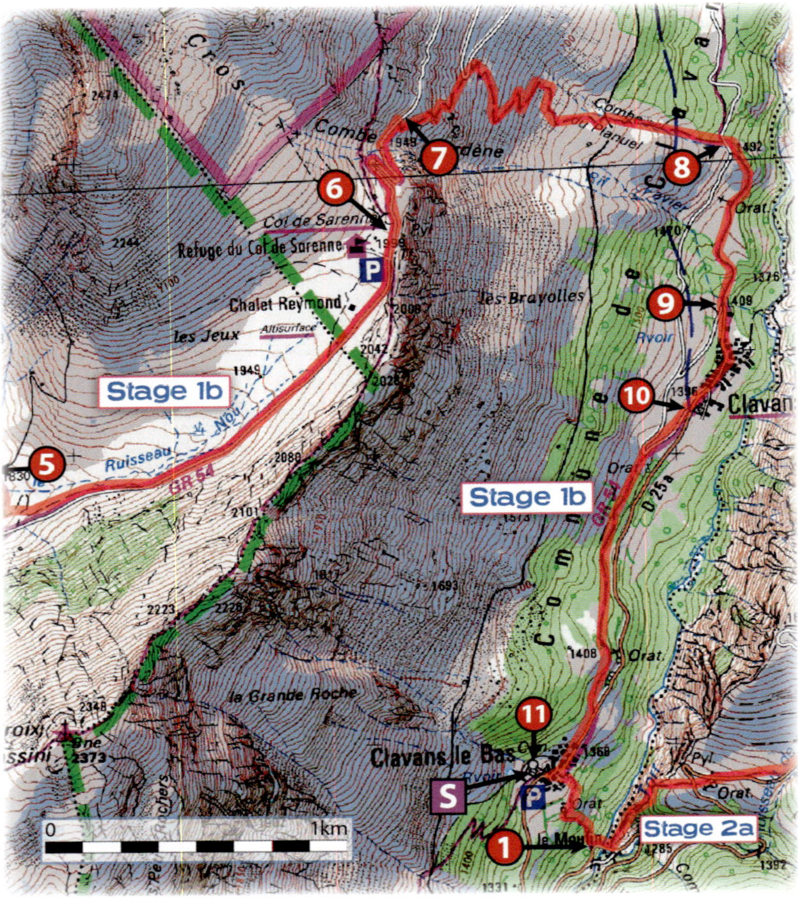

The beautiful, grassy landscape before Col de Sarenne

Clavans-le-Bas to Besse-en-Oisans

2a

The climb to Col de St-Georges (Stage 2b)

Descend to an old mill and then climb steeply to the immaculately preserved village of Besse-en-Oisans with its historic stone buildings. This is a great place to take a break or stock up on supplies.

Forest in Gorge de Sarenne (Stage 1b)

Time (hr:min)	1:00
Distance (km)	1.7
Ascent (m)	250
Descent (m)	60
Maximum altitude (m)	1550
Refreshments	Besse-en-Oisans
Accommodation	Besse-en-Oisans

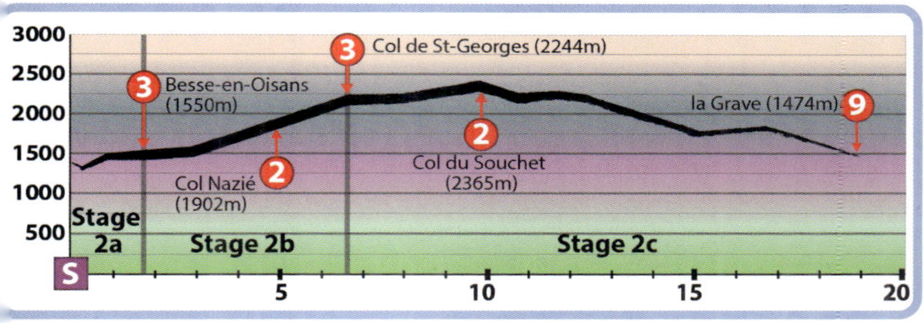

2a

The immaculately preserved stone buildings of Besse-en-Oisans

S From the telephone kiosk on Clavans' main street, descend on a tarmac lane ('Besse'), following waymarks. Continue descending steeply through forest.

1 0:10: TL onto a road. A few metres after an old mill, TL onto a steep path.

2 0:45 Cross over a road and continue upwards on a path ('Besse'). After a few minutes, TR onto a road. Soon TL onto a path. At the road again, walk up it. Shortly afterwards, TL onto a path ('Besse').

3 1:00: Cross a road to enter **Besse-en-Oisans (1550m)**. TL to head up the cobbled **Rue de Saint-Anne**. TR at the town hall and walk along the main street.

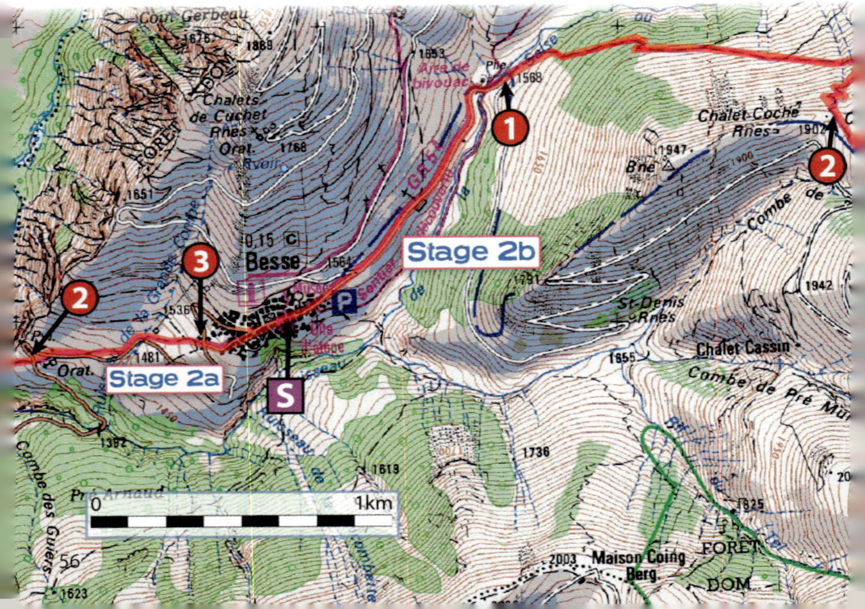

Besse-en-Oisans to Plateau d'Emparis

2b

The Plateau d'Emparis is a highlight of the ToE

A steep climb to one of the most scenic places in all of the Alps: the bucolic Plateau d'Emparis with its grandstand views of la Meije and its glaciers. On a fine day, this is a highlight of the ToE. There are a couple of refuges nearby, just off the ToE route: a fabulous place to spend the night.

Time (hr:min)	2:00
Distance (km)	4.9
Ascent (m)	694
Descent (m)	0
Maximum altitude (m)	2244
Refreshments	Refuges on Plateau d'Emparis
Accommodation	Refuges on Plateau d'Emparis

S Leave the village on the main road.

1 0:20: TR to cross a bridge and head E up a narrow road ('Plateau d'Emparis'). At the first hairpin bend, keep SH on a path.

2 1:15: At **Col Nazié (1902m)** keep SH ('Plateau d'Emparis') and continue climbing. Eventually, TR at a grassy col onto a track.

3 2:00: Shortly afterwards, just before a parking area, TL on a path to a signpost marking **Col de St-Georges (2244m)** which overlooks Plateau d'Emparis.

2c Plateau d'Emparis to la Grave

View of la Meije from Col de Sarenne

The balcony path directly in front of la Meije and its glaciers

Time (hr:min)	4:00
Distance (km)	12.4
Ascent (m)	400
Descent (m)	1181
Maximum altitude (m)	2365
Refreshments	La Grave
Accommodation	La Grave Le Chazelet Les Terrasses

A glorious traverse of the grazing slopes of the superlative Plateau d'Emparis is followed by a steep descent to the lovely hamlet of le Chazelet. The route continues descending all the way to the town of la Grave with its magnificent setting in front of la Meije. If you have the legs, consider the amazing side trip to Lacs Noir and Lérié (shown on the map below): on a clear day la Meije is reflected in the surface of the lakes.

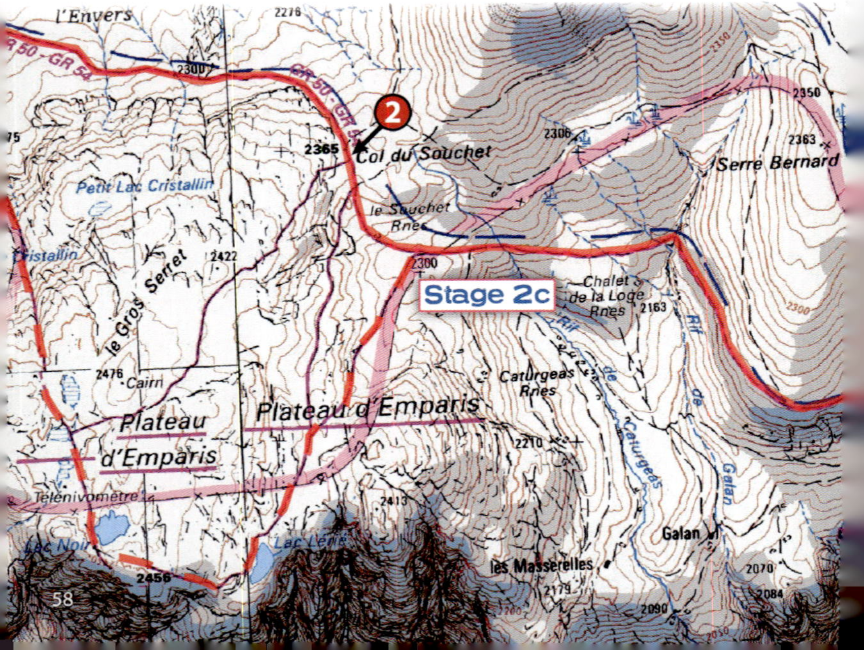

S From the signpost at **Col de St-Georges**, take the path running downhill ('Plateau d'Emparis').

1 0:20: Ford a stream and arrive at an information board. TR for the wonderful side trip to the lakes: join the ToE again S of **Col du Souchet**. Otherwise, keep SH on a path ('Col du Souchet') to the right of a track. Keep on the main path, ignoring offshoots.

2 1:00: Keep SH at **Col du Souchet (2365m)** ('le Chazelet'). Soon afterwards, keep SH at a junction ('le Chazelet').

3 2:10: Keep SH at a saddle and descend. After 10min, TR at a junction beside two benches ('le Chazelet').

4 2:50: At the base of a ski lift, TR to cross a bridge. Immediately afterwards, TR and climb on a track. Soon afterwards, keep SH at a junction.

5 3:00: At a junction in **le Chazelet (1786m)**, keep SH uphill. Exit the village through a car park and continue up the road ('la Grave'). Keep SH at the next junction.

6 3:20: At an exhilarating viewpoint (a plank jutting out over cliffs), TR onto a track now descending. Soon, the track crosses a road. Then at a confusing junction of paths and tracks, keep SH (E) to descend to the left of a house: note that a waymark incorrectly suggests you TR. At a road, TL.

7 3:30: At the first hairpin bend, TL onto a lane. Carefully follow waymarks down between the houses of **les Terrasses (1776m)**. Just below the village, TR onto a track. Shortly afterwards, TL and descend steeply on a grassy track. TR at a fork heading downhill. A few minutes later, TR onto another track.

8 4:00: Follow the waymarks down through **la Grave (1474m)**. Pass the church and descend to the main street.

3a la Grave to Villar d'Arêne

Villar d'Arêne

An easy walk (despite one climb) alongside the picturesque River Romanche to the spectacular village of Villar d'Arêne. There are superb views of la Meije on the way.

S Walk E along the main street of **la Grave**. Soon, TR onto a path descending between buildings. Soon, TL at a junction. Walk through the campsite to the **River Romanche**. TL and walk upstream.

1 0:20: Cross a bridge over the river. Immediately afterwards, TL ('Villar-d'Arêne'). Soon TR ('Villar-d'Arêne par la Forêt'). After a while, the path climbs steeply into the forest and then descends.

2 1:15: Arrive at a junction just beside **Villar-d'Arêne (1650m)**. To enter the village, TL, cross a bridge and climb briefly. To continue on the ToE instead, TR at the junction and climb.

Time (hr:min)	1:15
Distance (km)	3.4
Ascent (m)	340
Descent (m)	169
Maximum altitude (m)	1734
Refreshments	Villar-d'Arêne
Accommodation	Villar-d'Arêne

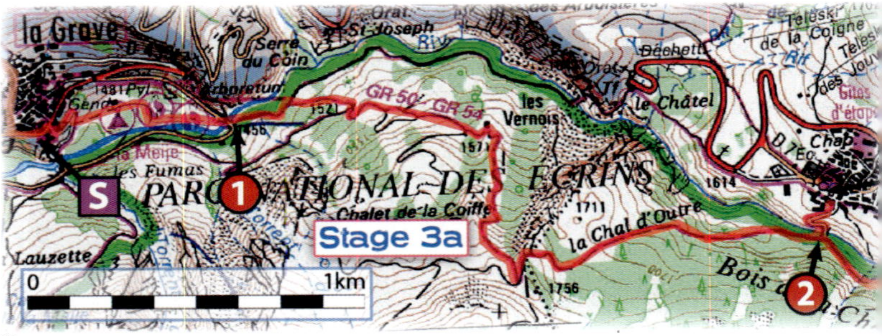

Villar d'Arêne to Pont d'Arsine

3b

A tranquil section of the River Romanche

A short peaceful stroll alongside the River Romanche to Pont d'Arsine. Often the sound of bells from the grazing cattle keeps the walker company. The gîte at Pont d'Arsine is a very nice place to stay and the food is excellent.

S From **Villar-d'Arêne**, retrace your steps back across the bridge to the junction. TL and climb briefly.

1 1:00: TL and cross **Pont des Brebis**. Then TR along a small road.

2 1:10: Arrive at **Pont d'Arsine (1667m)**.

Time (hr:min)	1:10
Distance (km)	2.8
Ascent (m)	85
Descent (m)	66
Maximum altitude (m)	1672
Refreshments	Gîte at Pont d'Arsine
Accommodation	Campsite and gîte at Pont d'Arsine

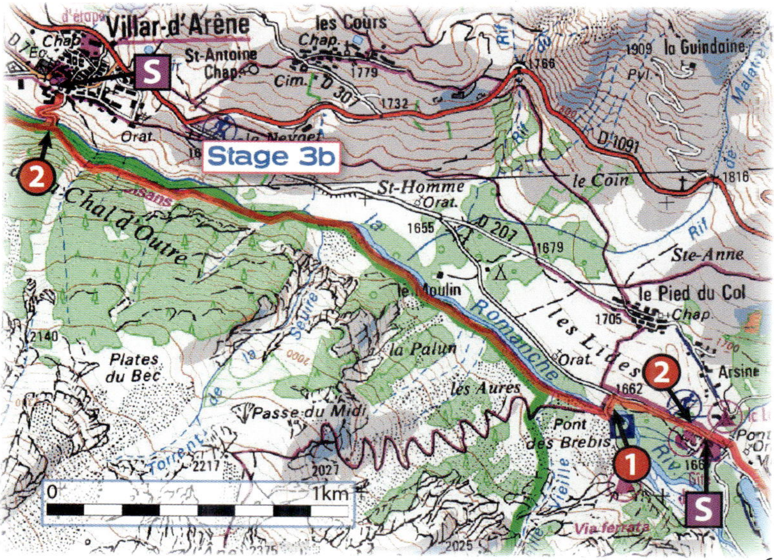

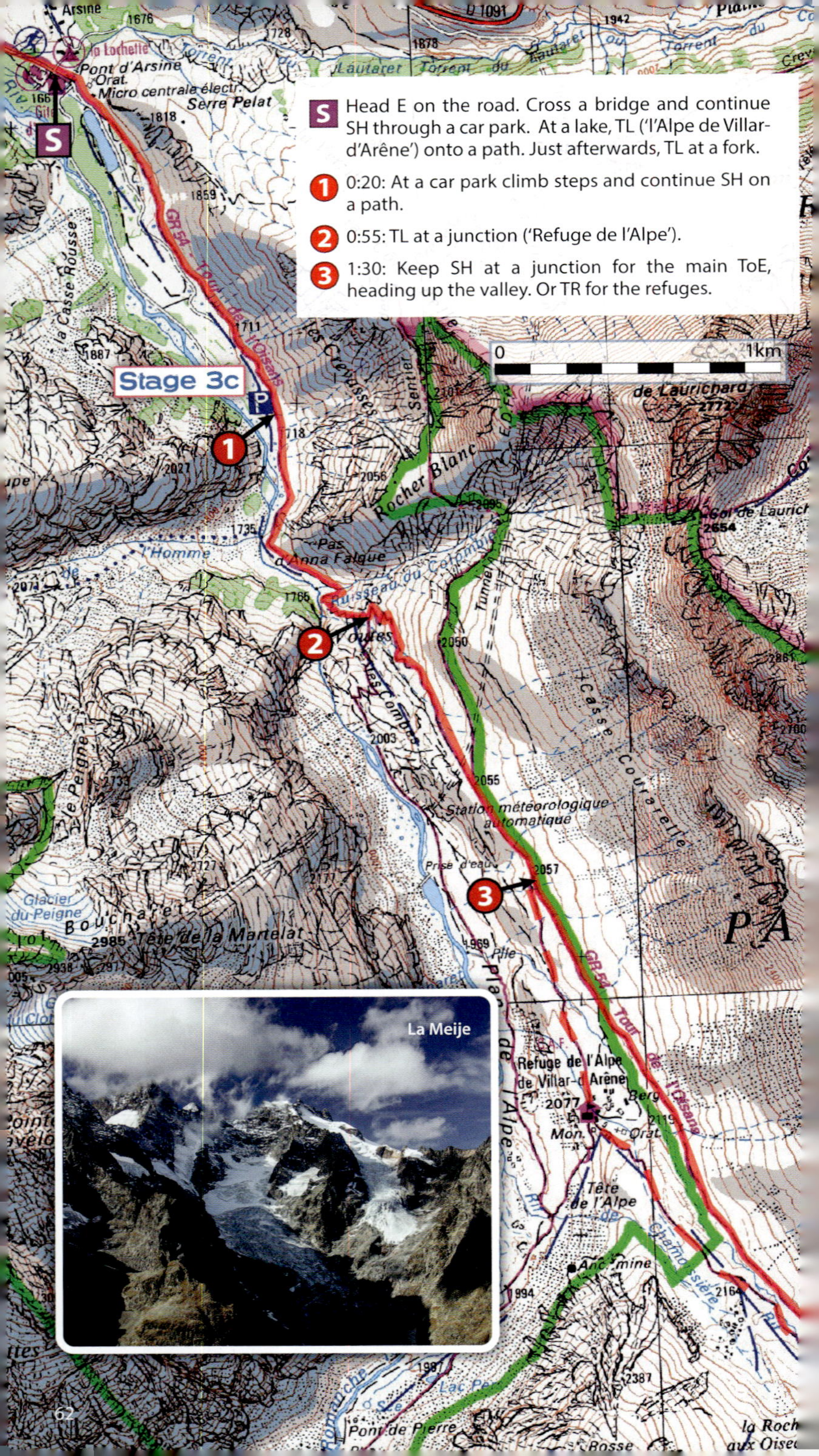

S Head E on the road. Cross a bridge and continue SH through a car park. At a lake, TL ('l'Alpe de Villar-d'Arêne') onto a path. Just afterwards, TL at a fork.

1 0:20: At a car park climb steps and continue SH on a path.

2 0:55: TL at a junction ('Refuge de l'Alpe').

3 1:30: Keep SH at a junction for the main ToE, heading up the valley. Or TR for the refuges.

Pont d'Arsine to le Monêtier-les-Bains

3c

Pic Gaspard seen on the gentle ascent to Col d'Arsine

A climb through the spectacular upper reaches of the Romanche Valley to Col d'Arsine, high up in the ENP with great views of the famous Montagne ces Agneaux. Descend past the stunning turquoise Lac de la Douche to the village of le Casset with its fascinating museum in an old mill. A short stroll along the River Guisane brings you to le Monêtier-les-Bains.

Time (hr:min)	5:00
Distance (km)	17.6
Ascent (m)	680
Descent (m)	877
Maximum altitude (m)	2340
Refreshments	Refuges at l'Alpe de Villar d'Arêne Gîte at le Casset Restaurants in le Monêtier-les-Bains
Accommodation	Refuges and camping at l'Alpe de Villar d'Arêne Gîte at le Casset Gîte, hotels & campsite at le Monêtier-les-Bains

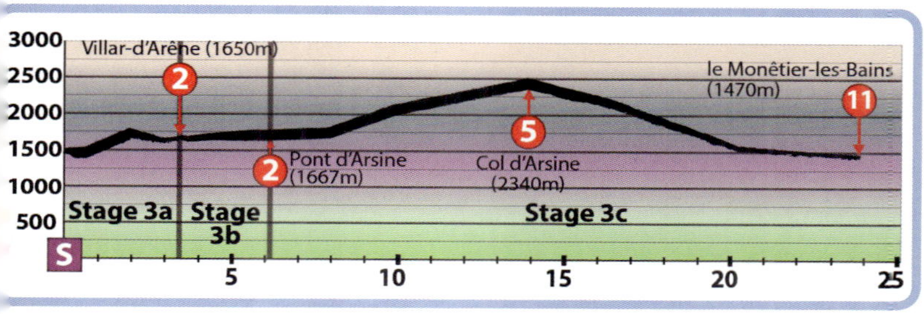

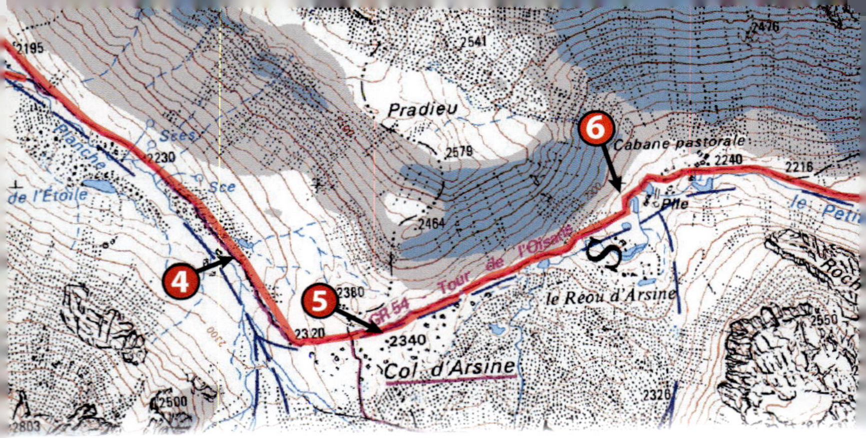

4 2:05: Keep SH (SE), ignoring a path heading upwards to the S. Shortly afterwards, cross some streams and continue SE. Soon the gradient increases.

5 2:20: Keep SH across the broad **Col d'Arsine (2340m)** and descend.

6 2:50: Pass some unnamed turquoise lakes.

7 3:45: Cross a footbridge at **Lac de la Douche (1901m)**. Just afterwards, TL on a rocky path. Soon descend through forest, ignoring offshoots.

8 4:15: TR, cross a bridge and descend on a track. There are short-cuts across some of the hairpins. Pass through a car park.

9 4:25: Cross a bridge into **le Casset (1512m)**. Immediately afterwards, TR along a street. TR to cross a bridge in front of a church. Beside the bridge is a museum in an old mill. TL immediately after the bridge onto a path which runs beside the river and then across pastures.

10 4:45: At a bridge, keep SH on the right bank of the river ('le Monêtier-les-Bains'). At a wide junction with a fork, keep right, passing between boulders to continue on the track. TL onto a path. Soon afterwards, TL onto a track. At a road beside a bridge, keep SH on a footpath, still on the right bank of the river.

11 5:00: Reach the spa baths in **le Monêtier-les-Bains (1470m)**.

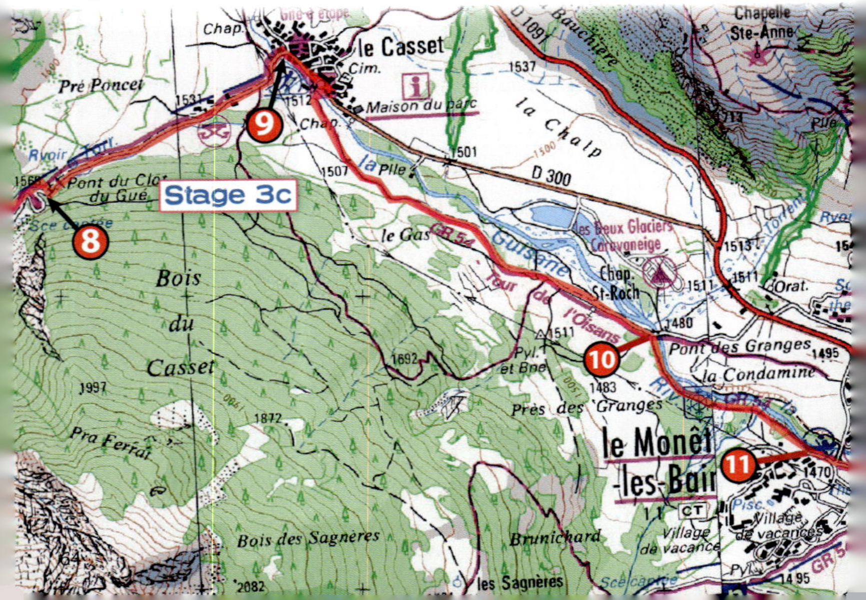

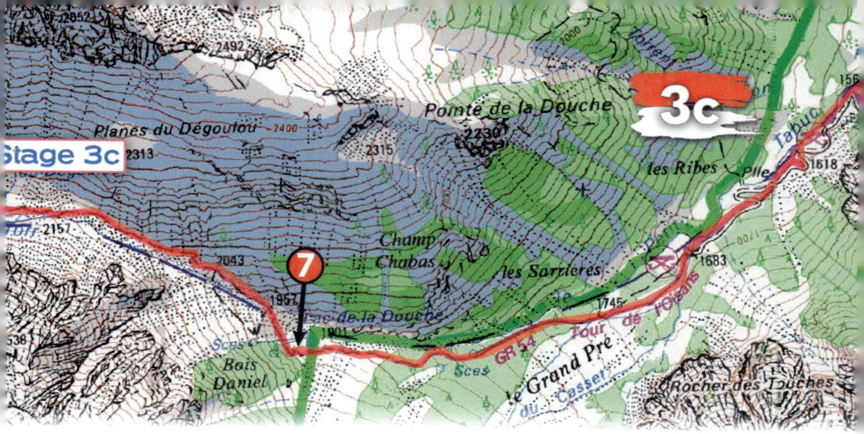

Lac de la Douche

4 le Monêtier-les-Bains to Vallouise

Descending from Col de l'Eychauda

After climbing through the forests around the ski resort of Serre Chevalier, cross Col de l'Eychauda and enter the beautiful pastures of the Eychauda Valley. Although much of the valley is in the ENP, it is still grazed during the summer and you get a taste of what life would have been like for shepherds in days gone by. Afterwards, descend into the Vallouise Valley enjoying wonderful views of Mont Pelvoux, one of the highest peaks in the ENP. A lovely river walk then brings you to the unforgettable village of Vallouise. The scenery is beautiful save for a short section passing ski infrastructure near the col.

Time (hr:min)	6:30
Distance (km)	19.6
Ascent (m)	955
Descent (m)	1262
Max. altitude (m)	2425
Refreshments	Buvette at Chambran; Vallouise
Accommodation	le Sarret; Vallouise

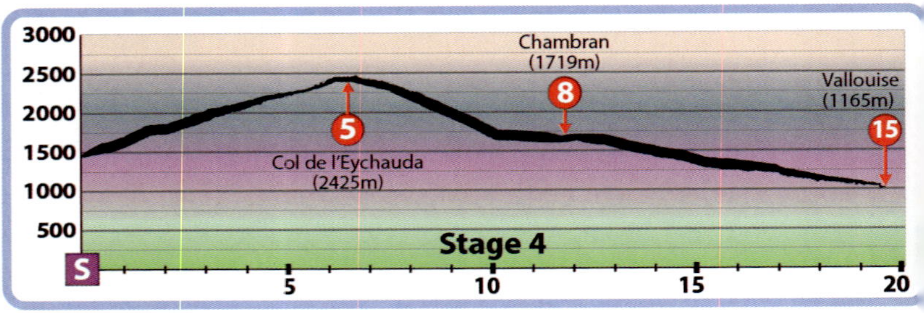

0
1km
le Monêtier-les-Bains
Pont des Granges
la Condamine
Granges
Bois des Sagnères
Brunichard
les Sagnères
Chap.
Village de vacances
Station
Charvet
Chap.
Torrent des Près les Fonts
les Grangettes
Stage v4
Stage 4
Tronchet
Clot Gaillard
la Grande Casse
Sce captée
GR 54
Tour de l'Oisans
Sentier de découverte
Bachas
le Bachas
Croix de Ciboult
Crête de Ciboult
Télésiège de Ciboult
Pas de l'Âne
Roche Peyron
Vallon de la Montagnolle
Pointe des Neyzets
Col du Vent
Col des Neyzets
Col des Grangettes
Roc de la Montagnolle
Col de la Montagnolle
Rocher de l'Yret
Col de l'Yret
Col de l'Eychauda
1
2
3
4
5
6
7

S From the footbridge to the S of the spa baths, head SE through a car park to a yellow signpost. Head SW on a track.

1 0:10: TL on a track ('Col de l'Eychauda'). Soon, TR onto a path. A few minutes later, TL at a fork.

2 0:30: TR in front of a **chapel**. Then TR at a junction. Shortly, TL ('le Bachas'). TR at the next junction. Soon keep SH ('le Bachas'). TL at another junction ('le Bachas'). Cross a stream. Immediately afterwards, TL at a fork. Shortly, cross the stream again (red and white waymarks) and walk up its right bank. TR to cross the stream again and continue on the path (yellow waymark). Soon afterwards, bear left and cross the stream one more time (yellow waymark).

3 2:00: TL at a signpost near the **Eychauda ski lift** and walk up a track. At the buildings of **le Bachas**, TR and climb on a track. After 10min, TR onto a path heading between trees. Shortly afterwards, ignore a path on the right and keep SH. Soon, TR onto the track again.

4 2:30: Keep SH at a junction.

5 3:00: Head across **Col de l'Eychauda (2425m)**. Soon afterwards, leave the track for a path heading S through a grassy plateau. Continue on the path as it zigzags downwards towards the **Eychauda Valley**.

6 4:00: Keep SH.

7 4:15: TL onto a track.

8 4:35: Keep SH on a road at **Chambran (1719m)**.

9 4:45: TR onto a rocky track ('Pelvoux'). Keep left at a fork onto a path, leaving the main track which descends more steeply.

10 5:05: Walk down a road. At the next hairpin bend, keep SH onto a path beside a chalet.

11 5:20: When you reach the road again, you have two options. For the original ToE route, TL and head S along the road and continue to follow these directions. For the new waymarked route which largely avoids the roads, see the box below.

12 5:45: TR onto a path (signposted 'Pelvoux-Le-Sarret').

13 5:55: TR onto a road. Immediately afterwards, TL to head downhill on another road.

14 6:00: TL at a T-junction to walk through the hamlet of **le Sarret**. After a few minutes, reach the **D994E**: TR and walk briefly up the road. After a few minutes, TL onto a track ('Vallouise'). TL at the river onto a path along its left bank.

15 6:30: Arrive at the village of **Vallouise (1165m)**.

New Stage 4 Route (avoiding roads)

The original Stage 4 route between 11 and Vallouise spends a lot of time on tarmac and is perhaps the least enjoyable part of the entire trek. It is welcome therefore that a new path has been introduced which largely avoids the roads: it is displayed in purple on our map. The new route adds 10-15min to Stage 4 but is much more pleasant.

From 11, follow a path NW. After 10min, turn sharp left at a junction and descend SE. After 5-10min, TR at another junction and descend SW to **le Riou**. Then continue SW, (now on a street). Soon TL along the **D994E**. Shortly afterwards, TR along a lane and cross a bridge over the **River Gyr**. Just afterwards, TL and follow a track downstream. Keep SH through the ski village of **Pelvoux**: ignore the first bridge. After a while, cross the river on a second bridge: immediately afterwards, TR on a path heading S along the riverbank: follow it all the way to **Vallouise (1165m)**.

Stage v4
Stage 4
Rocher de l'Yret
Col de la Montagnolle
Col de l'Yret
Crête des Neyzets
Crête de l'Yret
Ravin de la Montagnolle
la Sastrière
Ravin de la Sastrière
Coste du Laou
Vallon de Chambran
Seguret Foran
Ravin de Seguret Foran
Ravin des Avalanches
Ravin de la Plaine de St Jean
Riou la Selle
Mas de Fourchier
Cabane de Lerger
les Combaras
Cime des Crousagnes
Ravin du Pissa
Chambran
le Serre Blanc
les Prés du Rocher
Cabane
Coste Vieille
Ravin de Coste Plaras
Peyron des Cloux
Ravin du Cugulion
l'Eychauda
0
1km

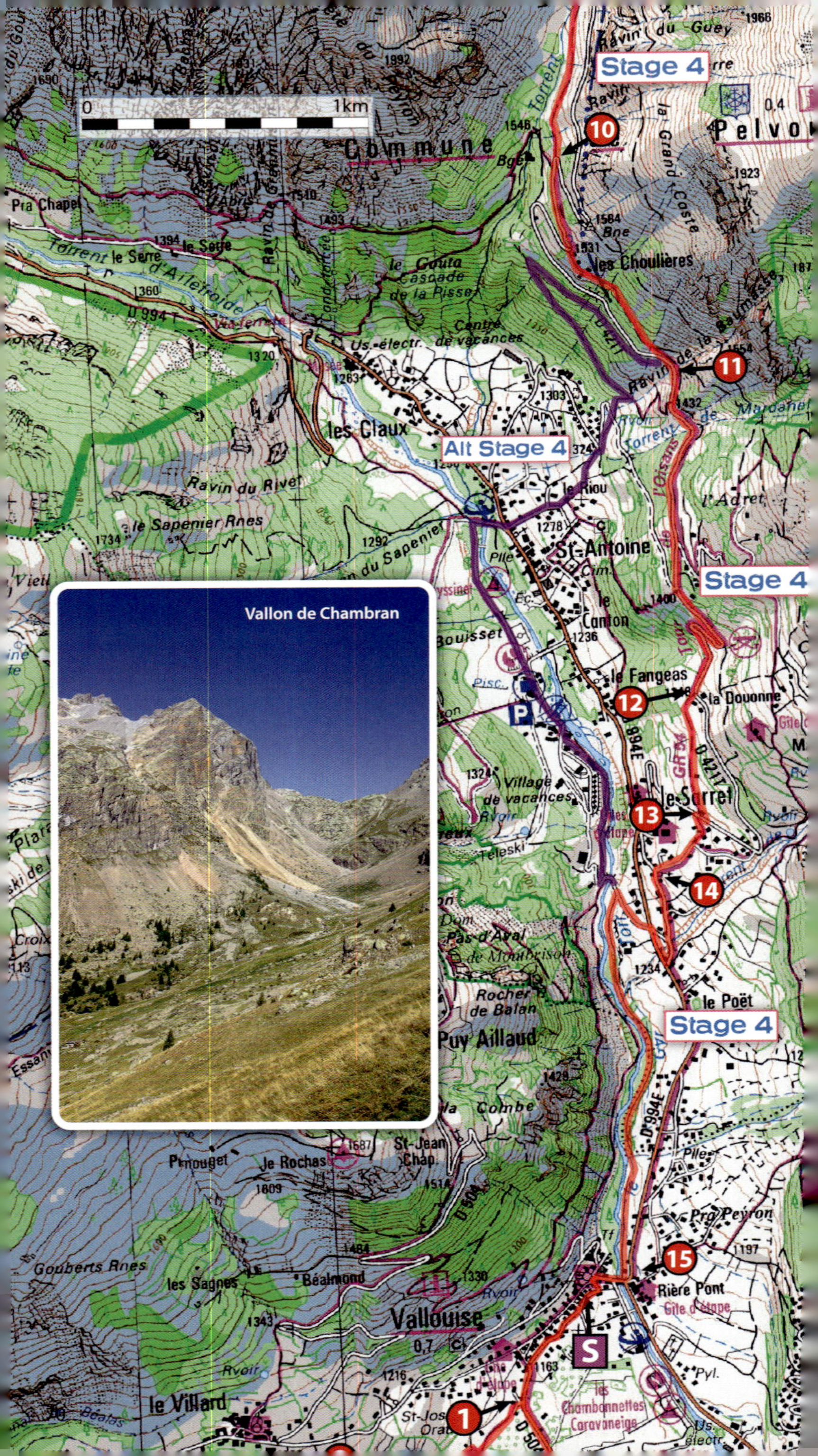

Vallon de Chambran

le Monêtier-les-Bains to Vallouise (via Col des Grangettes) v4

Lac de l'Eychauda

This incredible stage is not an official variant to the ToE. It is included here as a way of avoiding the ski infrastructure around Col de l'Eychauda. Although it is more challenging than the main ToE route, it is greatly superior. Firstly, it climbs the magnificent and rarely trodden Vallon du Grand Tabuc, well away from the ski slopes of Serre Chevalier. Then it crosses the exhilarating Col des Grangettes which is one of the finest cols in the region and far more beautiful than Col de l'Eychauda which is passed on Stage 4. From there, the incredible views of the icy turquoise Lac de l'Eychauda are a stark contrast to the warm grassy slopes of the valleys below. Purists may prefer to stick to Stage 4 but they will be missing out for Stage v4 is a gem.

The final part of the climb to Col des Grangettes is exposed and steep: some sections are protected by cable handrails. A fall here could have serious consequences so take care. There is also a short, steep, slippery section to descend just after the col. Navigation is relatively straightforward save that the path can be faint in Vallon du Grand Tabuc. Avoid the route in bad weather or low visibility.

Time (hr:min)	6:45
Distance (km)	21.6
Ascent (m)	1214
Descent (m)	1521
Max. altitude (m)	2684
Refreshments	Buvette at Chambran; le Sarret; Vallouise
Accommodation	le Sarret; Vallouise

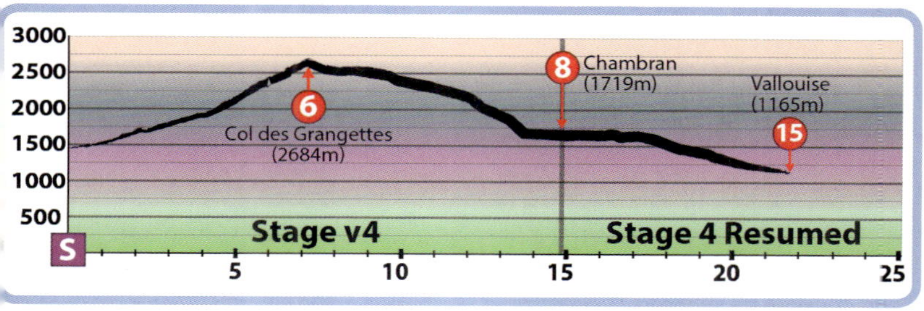

The grass in Vallon de Chambran turns a golden colour in autumn

S From the footbridge to the S of the spa baths, head SE through a car park to a yellow signpost. Head SW on a track.

1 0:10: Keep SH at a junction.

2 0:20: TR and cross a bridge. Then TL on a track. After 5min, keep SH on a path just to the right of a building.

3 0:40: Just after the hamlet of **les Grangettes**, TL on a path which descends to the river. TL and cross a footbridge over the river. Immediately afterwards, TR and climb on a track alongside the river. After a while, continue SH on a faint path which heads up the E side of **Vallon du Grand Tabuc**, close to the river.

4 1:25: Enter the **ENP**. Soon afterwards the path climbs SE up Vallon de la Montagnolle.

5 2:10: TR at a junction with a signpost ('Col des Grangettes') onto a path which heads SW across grass. Soon, climb up across a rocky slope and then zigzag steeply upwards. When the path becomes faint at the base of some crags, climb alongside them. Soon afterwards, TL at an orange waymark and climb steeply up through rocks towards a cable handrail which can be seen a few metres away. TR and climb alongside the handrail. Watch your footing as this section (and those that follow) are exposed. After the handrail, continue up through the rocks. The path is sometimes tricky to follow and there are further exposed sections with cables. From time to time, there are waymarks on the rocks.

6 3:00: Cross **Col des Grangettes (2684m)**. Descend steeply to the S, taking care on the loose rocks. Soon the path bends left and the gradient eases as you contour across the hillside towards the left of the lake below. Where the path disappears at some rocks, follow orange waymarks.

7 3:20: Follow more orange waymarks to a little saddle at the E tip of **Lac de l'Eychauda (2514m)**. Then follow cairns over rocks to find a path which heads initially E. Descend in a series of hairpins into the magnificent **Chambran Valley**.

8 4:50: Arrive at **Chambran (1719m)**. You are now back on the **main ToE** so follow the route of **Stage 4** to Vallouise.

Vallouise to Cabane du Jas-Lacroix 5a

Torrent des Bans at Entre-les-Aygues

Begin with a gentle climb alongside the tranquil River Onde. From Entre-les-Aygues, head into the magnificent Selle Valley with its fabulous cascades and clear blue rock pools. Enjoy expansive views of the surrounding peaks all the way to the remote unmanned Cabane de Jas Lacroix where you can spend the night if you are properly equipped. At the time of writing, there were sleeping bags, mats and basic cooking equipment in the cabane but it would not be wise to assume that these will be there on your arrival: bring your own sleeping bag, food and stove.

The walk to Entre-les-Aygues, some of which is on a narrow road, can be a little tiresome. It can be avoided by taking a taxi, or the morning shuttle from Vallouise which runs in the summer. The shuttle needs to be booked in advance: contact the Vallouise Tourist Office on +33 4 92 23 36 12.

Time (hr:min)	3:20
Distance (km)	13.1
Ascent (m)	820
Descent (m)	39
Max. altitude (m)	1946
Refreshments	None
Accommodation	Basic campsite at Pont des Places; Cabane du Jas Lacroix

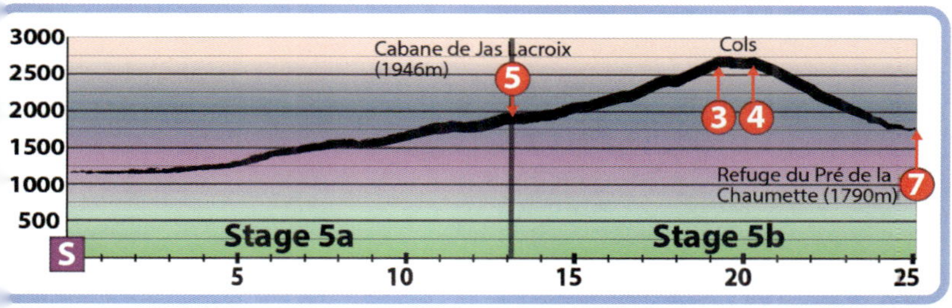

S From the fountain in the centre of Vallouise's main square, head S on 'Route Dessous Ville'. The street soon bends right. TR onto a road ('Pont des Fontaines'). A few minutes later, TL at a junction, remaining on the road.

1 0:10: TR onto a track called '**Chemin de la Pissette**' ('Pont des Fontaines'). Soon TR onto another track.

2 0:20: TL to cross **Pont des Fontaines**. TR immediately afterwards ('Pont des Places') and walk up the right bank of the **River Onde** on a track.

3 0:45: Arrive at **Pont des Places** where there is a **wild campsite** with basic facilities. Cross the bridge and TL to proceed up the road. There are some short-cuts across bends in the road.

4 2:00: TL at the W of the car park at **Entre-les-Aygues** ('Col de l'Aup Martin'). Shortly afterwards, TL again ('Col de l'Aup Martin'). Cross a footbridge over the **River Bans** and follow a path through trees. Then leave the trees and follow the path up the right side of the **Selle River**.

5 3:20: Just before **Cabane de Jas Lacroix (1946m)**, there is a fork. TL to head to the cabin. TR, following waymarks, to continue on the ToE.

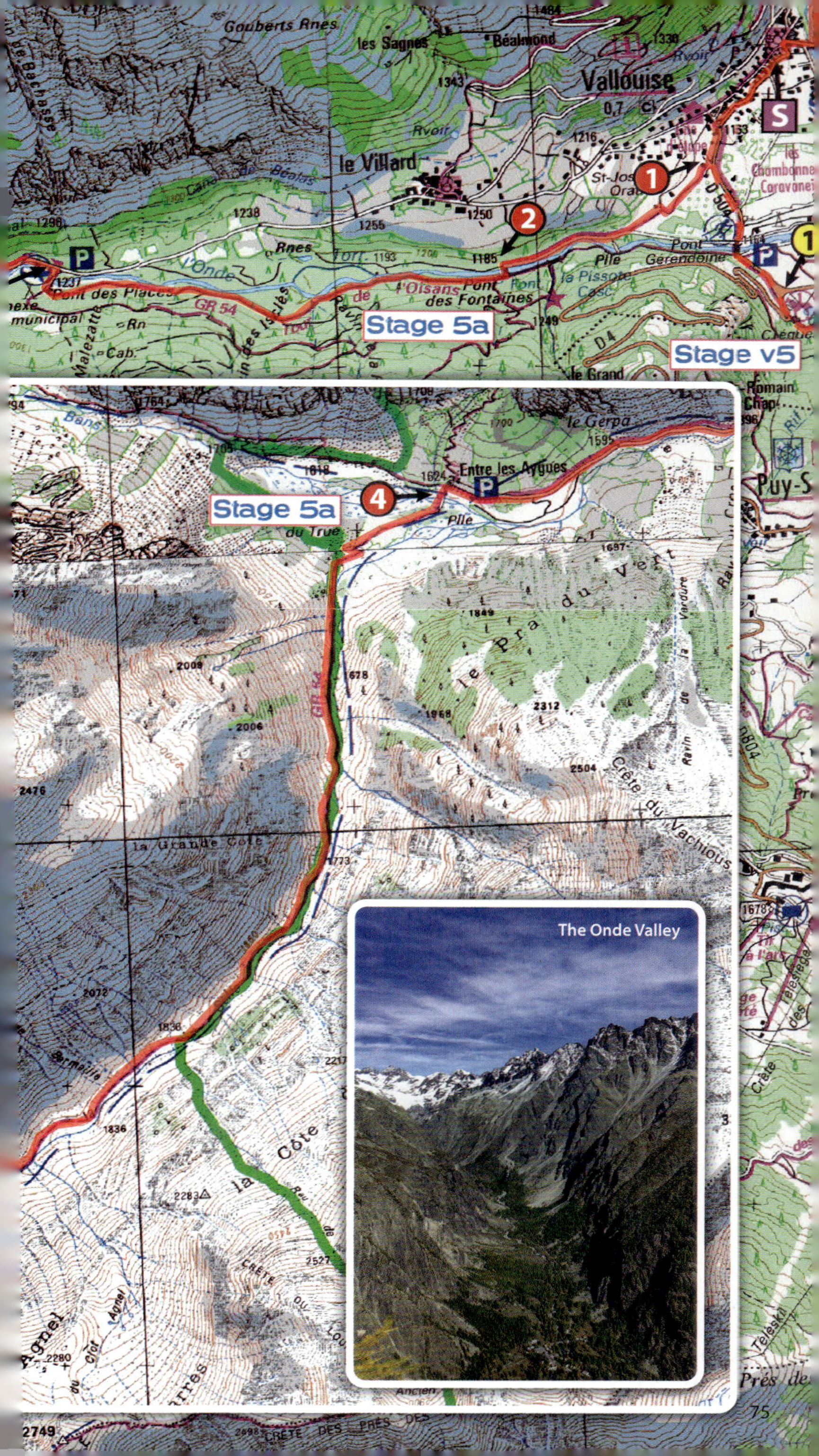

The Onde Valley

5b Cabane du Jas-Lacroix to Refuge du Pré de la Chaumette

Pas de la Cavale seen from the Champoléon Valley

This long, challenging stage is a highlight of the ToE, passing through a wild and remote part of the ENP. Two high and exposed cols are crossed and the views are exceptional.

The climb to Col de l'Aup Martin (the highest point on the ToE) is steep and exposed. The path is very narrow with some off-camber sections. The section between the cols is also exposed. A fall on these sections could have serious consequences. They can be slippery after rain or snow. The descent to the refuge is a real 'knee-jerker'.

Time (hr:min)	5:00
Distance (km)	11.9
Ascent (m)	830
Descent (m)	971
Max. altitude (m)	2761
Refreshments	Refuge du Pré de la Chaumette
Accommodation	Refuge du Pré de la Chaumette

Snow can lie near the cols into July and occasionally, new snow falls in summer. When snow melts and re-freezes, ice around the cols can be treacherous. And even a light dusting of snow can make the paths near the cols difficult to follow.

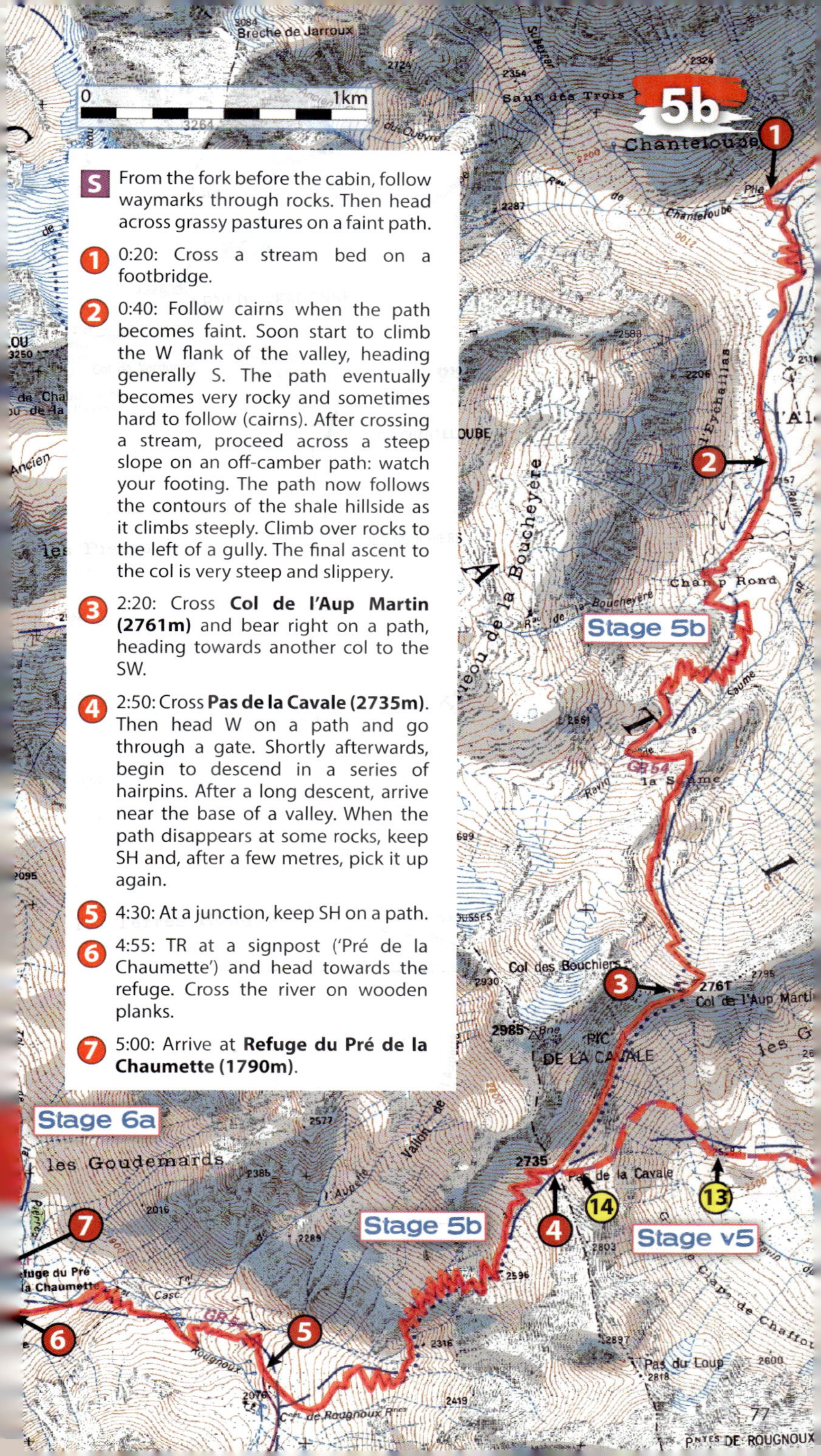

S From the fork before the cabin, follow waymarks through rocks. Then head across grassy pastures on a faint path.

1 0:20: Cross a stream bed on a footbridge.

2 0:40: Follow cairns when the path becomes faint. Soon start to climb the W flank of the valley, heading generally S. The path eventually becomes very rocky and sometimes hard to follow (cairns). After crossing a stream, proceed across a steep slope on an off-camber path: watch your footing. The path now follows the contours of the shale hillside as it climbs steeply. Climb over rocks to the left of a gully. The final ascent to the col is very steep and slippery.

3 2:20: Cross **Col de l'Aup Martin (2761m)** and bear right on a path, heading towards another col to the SW.

4 2:50: Cross **Pas de la Cavale (2735m)**. Then head W on a path and go through a gate. Shortly afterwards, begin to descend in a series of hairpins. After a long descent, arrive near the base of a valley. When the path disappears at some rocks, keep SH and, after a few metres, pick it up again.

5 4:30: At a junction, keep SH on a path.

6 4:55: TR at a signpost ('Pré de la Chaumette') and head towards the refuge. Cross the river on wooden planks.

7 5:00: Arrive at **Refuge du Pré de la Chaumette (1790m)**.

v5 Vallouise to Refuge du Pré de la Chaumette (via Col de la Pousterle)

This epic route is one of our favourites. It avoids the long slog up the Onde Valley on Stage 5a. However, at 11 hours, it is long and challenging. It used to be possible to break it up slightly with a stay at Refuge de la Pousterle (which needed to be booked in advance as it opened only on request) but at the time of writing the refuge had closed until further notice.

After a climb high above the Vallouise Valley, descend into, and walk the full length of, the unspoilt and little-known Fournel Valley. There are incredible views of snowy peaks all the way to Pas de la Cavale, and too many waterfalls to count. Late June is a particularly lovely time to undertake this route as the peaks on either side of the valley will still be thick with snow and there are few places in the whole of the Alps where the wild flowers are better. Indeed you will pass Réserve Biologique des Deslioures, the most important site in Europe for the rare and protected Chardon Bleu which flowers in summer.

Time (hr:min)	11:10
Distance (km)	30.3
Ascent (m)	1990
Descent (m)	1363
Max. altitude (m)	2735
Refreshments	None
Accommodation	Refuge de la Pousterle

After Deslioures the path is occasionally unstable and skirts close to the edge of steep cliffs so watch your footing. Also, sometimes the path is faint: there are waymarks and cairns. There are also some stream crossings: take care, particularly in spring when the volume of water is greater. After la Grande Cabane, the terrain becomes challenging and navigation skills are required: the path is faint and at times non-existent so follow cairns/waymarks. Shortly before the col, there is a steep climb up a shale slope: take care as a fall could be serious. Do not attempt this stage in low visibility or bad weather.

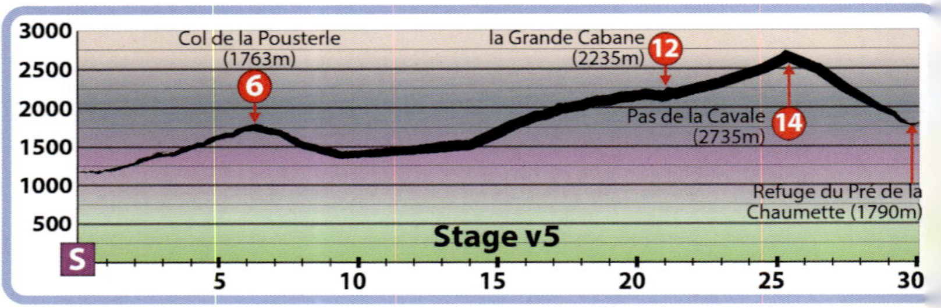

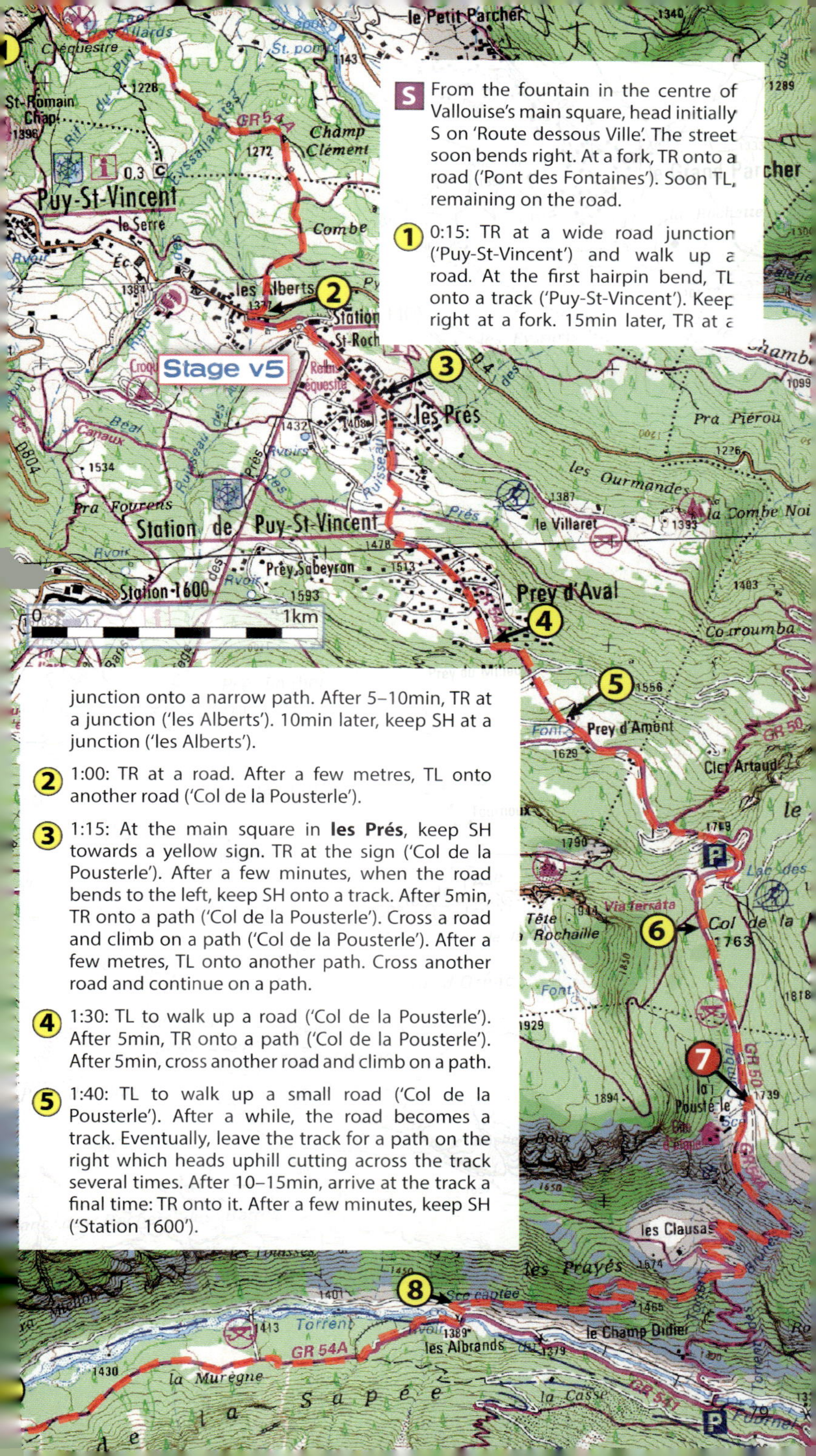

S From the fountain in the centre of Vallouise's main square, head initially S on 'Route dessous Ville'. The street soon bends right. At a fork, TR onto a road ('Pont des Fontaines'). Soon TL, remaining on the road.

1 0:15: TR at a wide road junction ('Puy-St-Vincent') and walk up a road. At the first hairpin bend, TL onto a track ('Puy-St-Vincent'). Keep right at a fork. 15min later, TR at a junction onto a narrow path. After 5–10min, TR at a junction ('les Alberts'). 10min later, keep SH at a junction ('les Alberts').

2 1:00: TR at a road. After a few metres, TL onto another road ('Col de la Pousterle').

3 1:15: At the main square in **les Prés**, keep SH towards a yellow sign. TR at the sign ('Col de la Pousterle'). After a few minutes, when the road bends to the left, keep SH onto a track. After 5min, TR onto a path ('Col de la Pousterle'). Cross a road and climb on a path ('Col de la Pousterle'). After a few metres, TL onto another path. Cross another road and continue on a path.

4 1:30: TL to walk up a road ('Col de la Pousterle'). After 5min, TR onto a path ('Col de la Pousterle'). After 5min, cross another road and climb on a path.

5 1:40: TL to walk up a small road ('Col de la Pousterle'). After a while, the road becomes a track. Eventually, leave the track for a path on the right which heads uphill cutting across the track several times. After 10–15min, arrive at the track a final time: TR onto it. After a few minutes, keep SH ('Station 1600').

6 2:10: Keep SH on the track across **Col de la Pousterle (1763m)** ('Vallon Fournel').

7 2:20: TR on a grassy track towards **Refuge de la Pousterle**. After a few metres, TL on a path heading S. When you meet the track again, walk down it. The track descends into the **Fournel Valley** in a long series of hairpin bends: occasionally there are short-cuts across the bends.

8 3:20: TL in the base of the valley onto another track. Shortly afterwards, TR at **les Albrands (1389m)**: descend briefly and cross a footbridge over the river ('Réserve Biologique'). Immediately afterwards, TR on a track. Meet another track and continue SH ('Bois Joli').

9 4:00: Pass a cabin on the right. Soon afterwards, keep SH past the bridge at **Boujurian** on a track ('Réserve Biologique'). Then pass a chalet on the right. Shortly afterwards, TR onto another path. After some time, pass a sign entering **Réserve Biologique des Deslioures (1560m)**. Cross a footbridge and continue on a wide path.

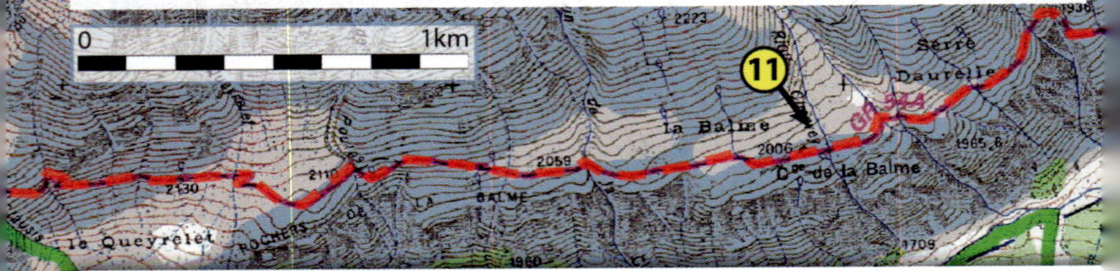

10 4:40: Arrive at a bridge over the river. The wild-flowers in the reserve on the left are incredible (see p78). TR and cross the bridge. Just afterwards, head NW to a nearby yellow signpost: follow the GR54A to the N ('la Grande Cabane') and immediately cross a ravine. Soon, the path heads W. After 5min, cross another ravine. Keep on the main route, ignoring offshoots. After descending into a ravine and crossing a stream, ignore a path to the left and continue to the right. Soon the path becomes faint as it heads up to the NW (waymarks). Shortly after a cairn, follow the path towards the SW through a boulder field and then cross a small stream to arrive back at a clear path.

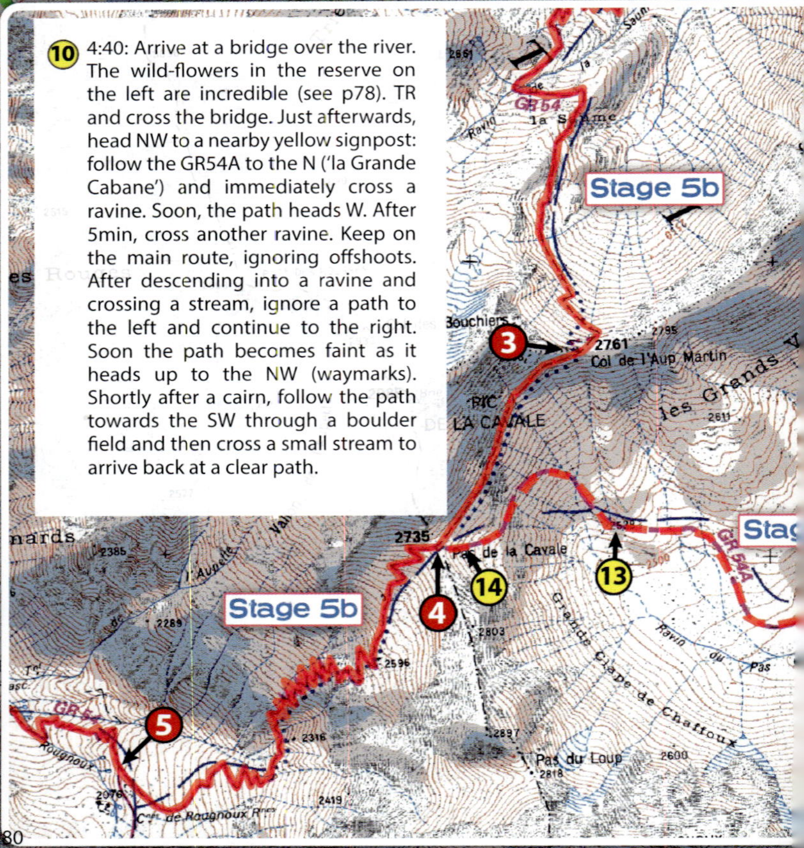

(11) 5:50: Pass above **Cabane de la Balme**. Keep on the main path heading across grassy slopes.

(12) 7:10: Approaching a cabin, the path heads across a grassy plateau and crosses streams. Then turn sharply left to descend to the river directly in front of **la Grande Cabane (2235m)**. Keep SH at a signpost opposite the cabin ('Pas de la Cavale'), still up the right side of the torrent: the path is faint at times but

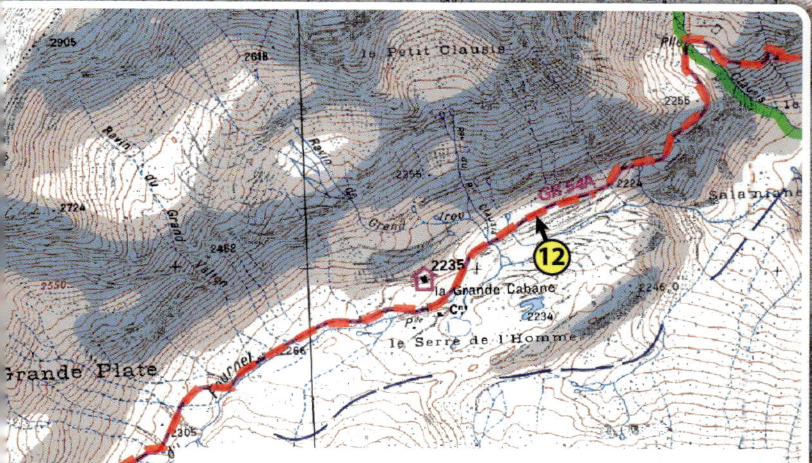

there are red/white waymarks. When the path disappears, follow cairns/waymarks/posts. After it reappears and disappears again, bear right up a slope (cairns/waymarks). Then bend left, traversing up across the slope. Soon, the route turns away from the torrent and heads into a huge mountain bowl. Follow cairns up alongside a stream bed.

(13) Eventually, approaching the cliffs at the head of the valley, the route becomes steeper and harder to follow. Climb a steep shale slope which heads up the right side of the cliffs: watch your footing as the drops are steep. Above the cliffs, briefly traverse on a grassy path. Then follow cairns and a shale path.

(14) 9:00: Cross **Pas de la Cavale (2735m)**. You are now back on the main ToE so follow the route of **Stage 5b** to the refuge.

From the west of the ENP, the Vercors range can clearly be seen

6a Refuge du Pré de la Chaumette to Refuge de Vallonpierre

Descending west from Col de la Valette

This unforgettable stage, entirely within a wild and remote part of the ENP, is another highlight of the ToE. Climb three exposed and spectacular mountain passes in quick succession: Col de la Vallette, Col de Gouiran and Col de Vallonpierre. The views are exceptional throughout but it is the peak of le Sirac (3441m) which dominates. The wonderfully situated Refuge de Vallonpierre is one of the most beautiful in the region

Time (hr:min)	4:50
Distance (km)	10.7
Ascent (m)	1190
Descent (m)	706
Max. altitude (m)	2668
Refreshments	Refuge de Vallonpierre
Accommodation	Refuge de Vallonpierre

There are some steep rock sections before Col de la Vallette: take care, particularly in early or late season if there is ice. The narrow shale paths descending from Col de la Vallette and Col de Gouiran can be slippery: a fall could have serious consequences. Snow can lie near the cols into July and occasionally, new snow can fall during summer. Even a light dusting of snow can make the paths near the cols difficult to follow.

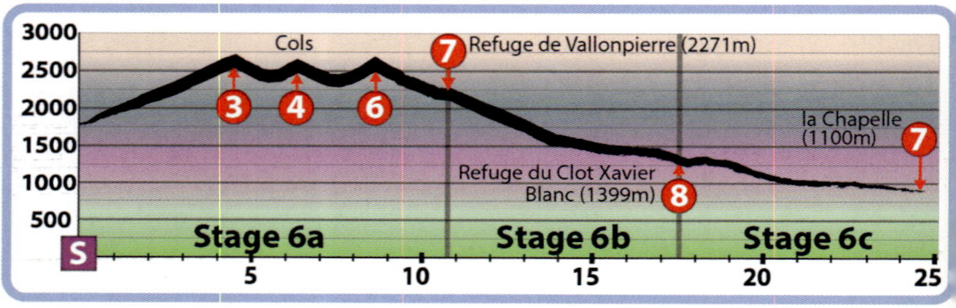

View from Vallon de Gouiran

6a
Stage 6b
Refuge de Vallonpierre
S
7
Lac de Vallonpierre
C.A.F.
l'Ocanière
Vallonpierre
Meyratte
le Peytrau
le Pré
Col du Roundeou
Stage 6a
Pic de Vallonpierre
6
Col de Vallonpierre
Mourière
Creux de Mourière
Ancien glacier de Gouiran
Vallon Plat
5
le Mourre de Clausis
3
4
Vallon de Gouiran
Col de Gouiran
4
Puy des Auberts
Puy des Agneaux
Tour du Vieux Chaillol
GR 54
2
1
P
Les Aubeas
Chaumette

S From the refuge, follow a path heading N into a valley. Soon start to climb the left flank of the valley across a shale slope.

1 0:35: The path bends to the left and climbs the slope to the W.

2 1:50: At approximately **2525m**, scramble up through a series of steep rocks, following waymarks.

3 2:15: Cross **Col de la Vallette (2668m)** with its magnificent 360° views. Descend the precipitous shale path on the other side. Cross through **Vallon de Gouiran**. Then climb in zigzags up the slopes to the W.

4 3:10: Cross **Col de Gouiran (2597m)** and descend on a shale path on the other side. Then contour around the hillside.

5 3:30: Above a grassy plateau, keep SH at a junction ('Col de Vallonpierre'). Note that this is where **Stage v6a** joins the main ToE. Continue traversing around the slopes and then climb steeply.

6 4:10: Cross **Col de Vallonpierre (2607m)**. Then descend on the path on the other side of the col.

7 4:50: Arrive at **Refuge de Vallonpierre (2271m)**. At the junction before the refuge, keep SH.

v6a Refuge du Pré de la Chaumette to Refuge de Vallonpierre (via Vallon d' Isola)

A fabulous, little-trodden alternative to the true ToE. Start with a lovely descent through the Champoléon Valley. Then climb the beautiful and peaceful Isola valley to the bucolic Vallon Plat where you rejoin the main ToE. Climb Col de Vallonpierre and finally descend to Refuge de Vallonpierre with its amazing setting beside a pretty lake on a huge grassy plateau.

The path on the ascent through the Isola valley is often narrow, unstable and exposed. And there are sections where you will need to scramble up exposed rocks so this route requires a good head for heights. Navigation through this valley can also be a little tricky. Some suggest that this stage is a bad weather alternative to Stage 6a: however, although it avoids Col de la Vallette and Col de Gouiran, the high, exposed Col de Vallonpierre (2607m) still needs to be crossed and the rocky scrambling in Vallon d'Isola would not be pleasant in wet weather or low visibility.

Time (hr:min)	4:50
Distance (km)	12.7
Ascent (m)	1167
Descent (m)	686
Max. altitude (m)	2607
Refreshments	Refuge de Vallonpierre
Accommodation	Refuge de Vallonpierre

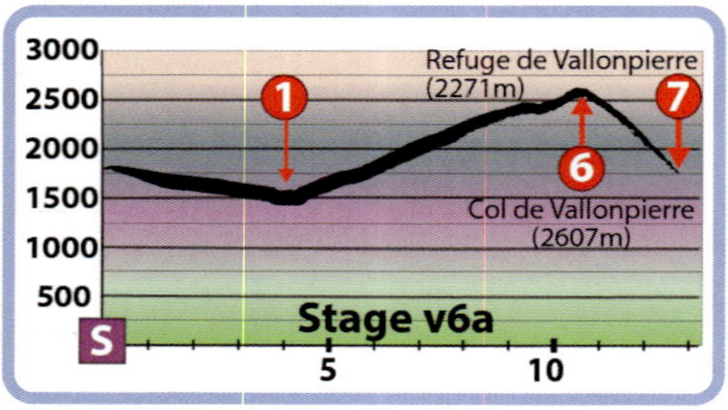

View from the slopes of the Isola valley

S Pick up a grassy path to the W of the refuge running down the **Champoléon valley**. After a few minutes, TR at a fork. Shortly afterwards, keep SH at a signpost ('les Auberts') and the path climbs briefly into the forest. Soon, descend in and out of the trees.

1 1:00: TR at a junction near a bridge (signposted 'les Auberts'). Shortly afterwards, TR onto a small path ('Col de Vallonpierre'). Quickly, the path rises above the Champoléon valley and enters the **Isola valley**.

2 1:30: The rocky path climbs N up the E side of the valley. Then it bends left, heading directly into the valley again, along the foot of some cliffs. There are now many exposed sections where you will need to climb along or over rocks. At the time of writing, some new bolts had been fixed into the rocks on some of the most exposed sections so the intention may be to mount cable handrails.

3 2:30: The path zigzags up to the E and heads through a grassy plateau where the path is faint. Arrive directly beside some steep cliffs with a lovely waterfall. Take care not to get too close to the edge. Continue climbing on the path and soon there are more sections of rocks to be climbed, although not as exposed as before. After a while, cross a slightly unstable shale slope. Watch your footing as the drops are steep.

4 3:15: Shortly afterwards, arrive at a huge plateau where there are usually sheep grazing. Cross some rocky stream beds. Shortly afterwards, TR and leave the path to head NE up a grassy spur.

5 3:30: After a few minutes, TL at a signpost to rejoin the main ToE ('Col de Vallonpierre'). Traverse the slopes on a path and then climb steeply.

6 4:10: Cross **Col de Vallonpierre (2607m)**. Then descend on the path on the other side of the col.

7 4:50: Arrive at **Refuge de Vallonpierre (2271m)**. At the junction before the refuge, keep SH.

6b Refuge de Vallonpierre to Refuge du Clot-Xavier Blanc

Refuge de Vallonpierre is set in a beautiful hanging valley

A long descent into the beautiful Séveraisse Valley finishes at the pretty Refuge du Clot Xavier Blanc. On a fine day, the scenery is sublime so this is not a stage to be rushed.

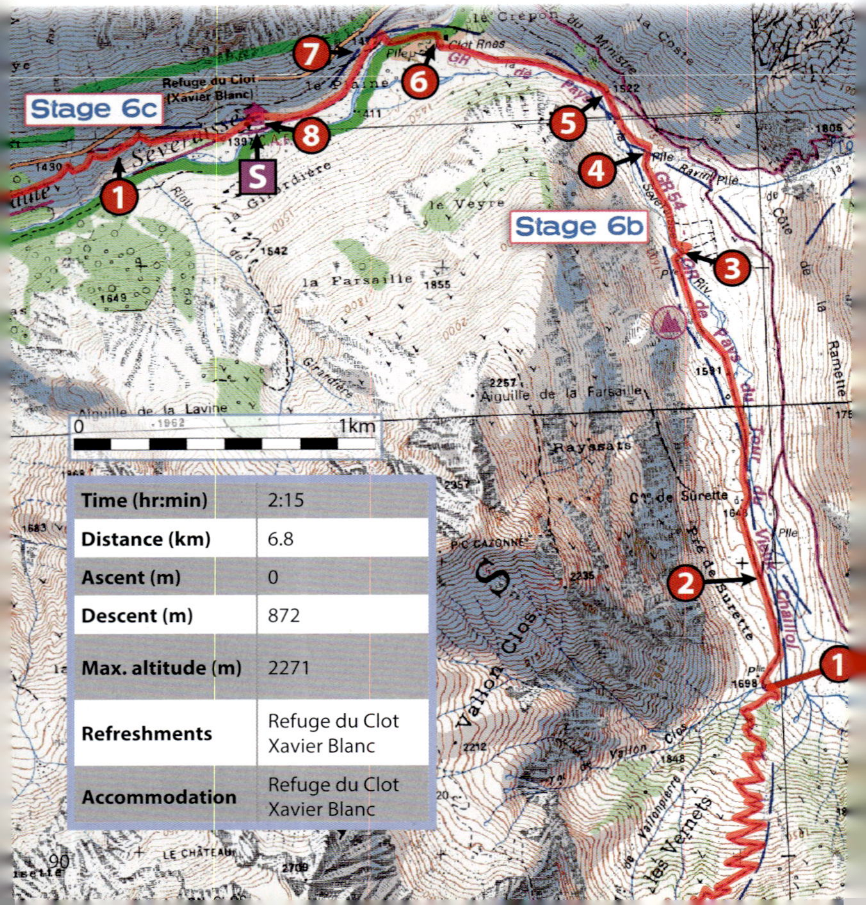

Time (hr:min)	2:15
Distance (km)	6.8
Ascent (m)	0
Descent (m)	872
Max. altitude (m)	2271
Refreshments	Refuge du Clot Xavier Blanc
Accommodation	Refuge du Clot Xavier Blanc

S From the refuge, proceed to the E side of the lake. Then head E to a signpost: keep SH ('la Chapelle'). Shortly afterwards, TR at a junction, following cairns. The path descends through carpets of alpenrose (which flower in June/July) and myrtle bushes (a relative of the blueberry which bears edible fruit in late summer).

1 1:10: Cross a footbridge over a torrent.

2 1:15: Keep SH at a junction ('la Chapelle'). A few minutes afterwards, keep SH at a faint junction (waymark on a rock). Just afterwards pass **Cabane de Surette**.

3 1:35: Cross a footbridge.

4 1:45: Cross another footbridge. Then TL on the path heading down the valley.

5 1:50: Keep SH at a junction with a signpost.

6 2:00: Walk between dry-stone walls to a pass a chalet. Immediately afterwards TR and cross a footbridge. Then TL and follow the path heading down the right bank of the **Séveraisse River**.

7 2:05: TL at a junction (signposted 'la Chapelle').

8 2:15: Arrive at **Refuge du Clot-Xavier Blanc (1399m)**.

A morning inversion seen on the descent

6c Refuge du Clot-Xavier Blanc to la Chapelle-en-Valgaudemar

A long but gentle stroll alongside the River Séveraisse, passing the historical hamlets of le Rif du Sap and le Bourg. Finish in the pretty village of la Chapelle-en-Valgaudemar which is a lovely place to stay. Stock up your supplies here as there are no more shops until le Bourg d'Oisans.

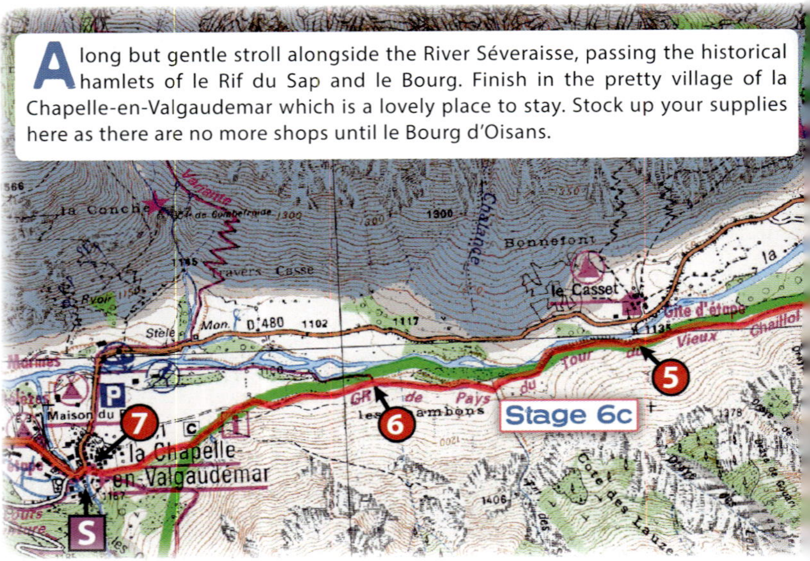

S From the refuge, head W on a path.

1 0:05 TL at a junction ('la Chapelle').

2 0:20: Pass between the houses of the pretty little hamlet of **le Rif du Sap**. Shortly afterwards ford a stream on boulders.

3 0:45: TR onto a wide track.

4 1:00: TL to cross a bridge. Then keep SH on a track to the hamlet of **le Bourg**. Head up through the hamlet, following waymarks. After the fountain, TR at a fork. After leaving the hamlet, continue SW on a path.

5 1:20: Keep SH at a junction by an old bridge ('la Chapelle').

6 1:35: TL at a junction onto a path. Pay attention here as the confusing signpost indicates that la Chapelle is SH rather than left.

7 1:45: Pass down between houses to enter the village of **la Chapelle (1100m)**.

La Chapelle-en-Valgaudemar

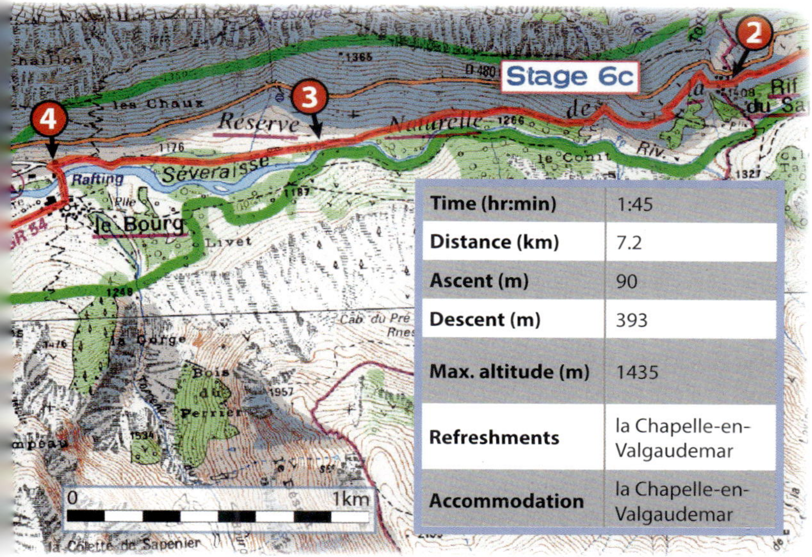

Time (hr:min)	1:45
Distance (km)	7.2
Ascent (m)	90
Descent (m)	393
Max. altitude (m)	1435
Refreshments	la Chapelle-en-Valgaudemar
Accommodation	la Chapelle-en-Valgaudemar

7a la Chapelle-en-Valgaudemar to Villar Loubière

Another gentle walk alongside the River Séveraisse leads to the village of Villar Loubière with its fabulously preserved old mill.

Time (hr:min)	1:00
Distance (km)	4.5
Ascent (m)	0
Descent (m)	67
Max. altitude (m)	1100
Refreshments	None
Accommodation	Campsite at Villar Loubière

View from the path to Villar Loubière

S Head W along the road out of la Chapelle.

1. 0:05: TR and cross a bridge. Immediately afterwards, TL on a track. After 15min, at a junction, keep left on a grassy track alongside the river which soon becomes a path.
2. 0:25: TL and cross a footbridge. Then follow a track along the left bank of the river.
3. 0:40: At the village of **les Andrieux**, cross the main road and then TR ('Villar-Loubière') onto a track.
4. 0:45: TR at a junction ('Villar-Loubière').
5. 0:55: TR at a junction and cross a bridge. Then TL and walk along the main road.
6. 1:00: Enter the village of **Villar-Loubière**. When the road bends sharply left, keep SH up a little street between stone buildings to arrive at the old mill.

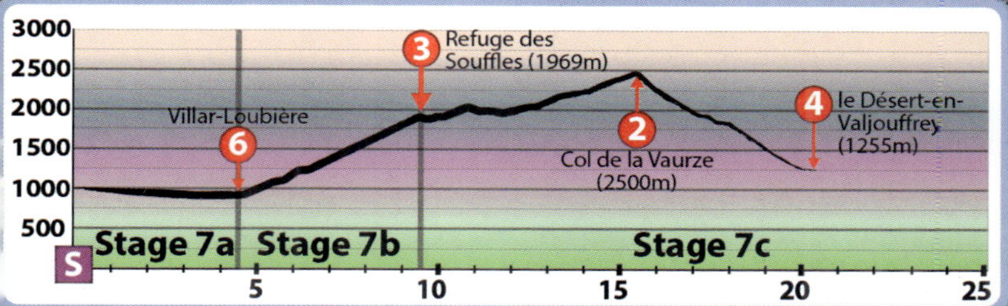

7b Villar Loubière to Refuge des Souffles

A relentless but magnificent climb to Refuge des Souffles with its spectacular setting below Pic des Souffles (3098m), Cime d'Orgières (3061m), Pic Turbat (3028m) and the famous peak of l'Olan (3564m). Sections of the route pass close to the edge of high cliffs so take care.

Time (hr:min)	2:30
Distance (km)	5
Ascent (m)	952
Descent (m)	0
Max. altitude (m)	1969
Refreshments	Refuge des Souffles
Accommodation	Refuge des Souffles

S Pass in front of the old mill and climb to a tarmac lane. TR and walk up the lane. At a junction with a fountain, TL and climb on a tarmac lane. Shortly after **Gîte la Charrière**, TL at a junction ('Refuge des Souffles'). The path now winds its way relentlessly upwards, often passing precipitously close to the edge of cliffs.

1 1:00: The path descends briefly. Just where it starts to rise again, keep right at a fork.

2 1:30: TL at a junction ('Refuge des Souffles').

3 2:30: TR at a junction and climb for a few minutes to **Refuge des Souffles (1969m)**.

Refuge des Souffles to le Désert-en-Valjouffrey

7c

Part of the amazing 360° panorama from Col de la Vaurze, including the magnificent peak of l'Olan

A lengthy traverse through incredible alpine scenery is followed by a long but rarely steep climb to Col de la Vaurze. With its far-reaching 360° views, the col is one of the best places from which to view the spectacular peak of l'Olan (which dominates the stage). Golden eagles and vultures are often spotted in this area. A long knee-jerking descent follows, all the way to the remote hamlet of le Désert-en-Valjouffrey.

On the traverse, there are short sections where the route crosses rocky gullies with torrents running down them: the drops are steep and the path is narrow so take care. Snow can lie near the col into July and occasionally, new snow falls in summer. When snow melts and re-freezes, ice around the col can be treacherous. And even a light dusting of snow can make the paths difficult to follow. The first section of the descent from the col is very steep and can be slippery after rain or snow.

Time (hr:min)	4:30
Distance (km)	10.8
Ascent (m)	648
Descent (m)	1358
Max. altitude (m)	2500
Refreshments	Le Désert
Accommodation	Le Désert

S Head N from the refuge on a path. After a few metres, TL at a signpost ('Col de la Vaurze') and descend to a junction just below the refuge: head NW on a path contouring around the hillside ('Col de la Vaurze').

1 1:30: After a long undulating traverse, the climb to the col begins. The path zigzags upwards for ages but the gradient is rarely very steep. There is a short section of scree to cross. When the path disappears at some rocks, climb around them and rejoin the path (waymark).

2 2:35: Cross **Col de la Vaurze (2500m)** and follow the path, zigzagging steeply down the other side.

3 3:35: The path levels and becomes faint as it passes through a section of boulders: follow cairns. Soon descend steeply again.

4 4:30: Cross a bridge and climb briefly on a track to enter **le Désert-en-Valjouffrey (1255m)**.

Stage 8a
Stage 7c
Combe des Marmes
la Roche
Petite
Anc. Ardoisières
Sce captée
le Désert en Valjouffrey
les Charmettes
S
P
Cim.
Gîte d'étape
Pont de la Bonne
Sources de la Bonne
Côte du Rif
Tête de l'Essart
les Fouches
Bonne
Anc. Ardoisières
Ruisseau
Rau de Serveille
Cabane de Serveille
les Soufflons
les Echarennes
les Blaches
Col de la Vaurze
le Collet
l'Homme Mort
Tête du Clotonnet
Stèle
0
1km
1973
1684
1574
1995
1363
1362
1309
1292
1307
1252
1266
1179
1451
1837
1885
1807
2085
1716
1949
2005
1921
1941
2667
2500
2683
2730
2710
2268
1
2
3
4
le Désert-en-Valjouffrey

Le Désert-en-Valjouffrey to Valsenestre

8a

The glorious descent towards Valsenestre

Climb to Col de Côte Belle, with its beautiful views of the Valjouffrey and Béranger valleys. Then descend to the immaculately preserved Valsenestre, perhaps the finest hamlet in the region. This beautiful stage is almost entirely within the boundaries of the ENP. It can be undertaken on its own with a stay in Valsenestre or it can be doubled up with Stage 8b (avoiding Valsenestre). The latter option makes for a challenging day. A stay in Valsenestre is essential for walkers attempting the stunning Stage v8b variant.

Take care on the descent as the path runs precipitously along the edge of extremely steep cliffs. Look out for the interesting schist formations in and around the col. Note that the elevation profile below excludes the trip from the junction at waymark 6 to Valsenestre.

Time (hr:min)	3:55
Distance (km)	11.2
Ascent (m)	1050
Descent (m)	988
Max. altitude (m)	2290
Refreshments	Valsenestre
Accommodation	Valsenestre; Official wild camp site just E of Valsenestre

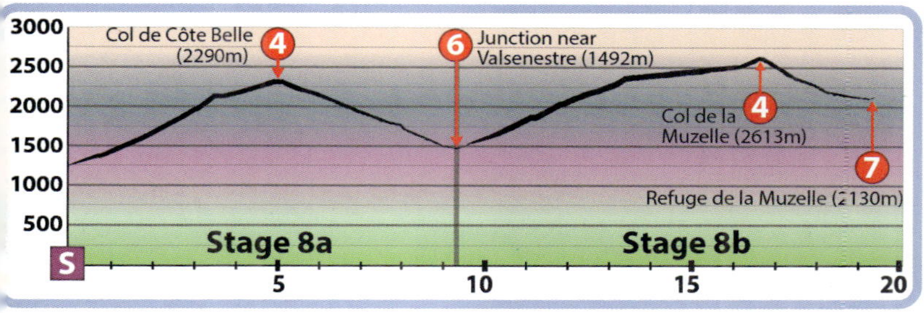

8a

S From a junction near the bridge crossed at the end of Stage 7c, head up a road ('Col de Côte Belle'). Shortly, keep SH to climb on a tarmac lane which soon becomes a track. TL at an ENP sign and climb on a path. Soon descend briefly to a stream and then climb alongside it.

1 0:20: Cross over the stream bed and continue uphill on the other side.

2 1:05: The gradient increases and the path ascends in a series of hairpins. Stick to the main path to avoid erosion of the slopes.

3 1:50: The gradient eases and the path makes long traverses back and forth across the hillside.

4 2:30: Cross **Col de Côte Belle (2290m)** and descend the path on the other side.

5 3:25: TR onto a track and continue descending.

6 3:30: keep SH at a **junction (1492m)** to head to Valsenestre. Alternatively, TR if you are continuing on Stage 8b and climb on a track ('Col de la Muzelle').

7 3:55: TR to enter **Valsenestre (1294m)**.

The approach to Col de Côte Belle

Valsenestre to Refuge de la Muzelle

8b

Sheep grazing below Col de la Muzelle

Another spectacular outing through a remote part of the ENP. The climb to Col de la Muzelle is tough but the scenery is as fine as any on the ToE. After crossing the col, descend to Refuge de la Muzelle which is beautifully set in a mountain cirque overlooking Lac de la Muzelle. The stage can be undertaken on its own, after a stay at Valsenestre, or it can be doubled up with Stage 8a (avoiding Valsenestre). The latter option makes for a challenging day.

Time (hr:min)	4:15
Distance (km)	11.9
Ascent (m)	1340
Descent (m)	493
Max. altitude (m)	2613
Refreshments	Refuge de la Muzelle
Accommodation	Refuge de la Muzelle

The last 300m (altitude) of the climb are very steep and exposed and can be muddy and slippery after rain or snow. Take care also on the steep descent from the col. Snow can lie near the col into July and occasionally, new snow can fall during summer. Even a light dusting of snow can make the paths near the col difficult to follow. Do not approach the Patous which operate in this area (see Introduction).

v8b Valsenestre to la Danchère

Lac Labarre and Signal du Lauvitel seen from Tête des Chetives

The scenery offered up by this official ToE variant is outstanding. It is a fine, if demanding, alternative to Stage 8b, particularly if Refuge de la Muzelle is full. It climbs through pastures to the beautiful Lac Labarre and then makes a long traverse on a wonderful balcony path. A second climb to the magnificent viewpoint of Brèche du Périer is then followed by a long knee jerking descent.

The route is long and challenging. However, it could possibly be broken with a stay at the unmanned Cabane de la Selle: it is not clear whether this is permitted but stays of one night may be tolerated. The phone number is (0)476302047 but making contact is difficult. Parts of the route are exposed so take care. The descent from Brèche du Périer is tricky.

Time (hr:min)	9:45
Distance (km)	20.5
Ascent (m)	1646
Descent (m)	1951
Max. altitude (m)	2491
Refreshments	la Danchère
Accommodation	Gîte at la Danchère

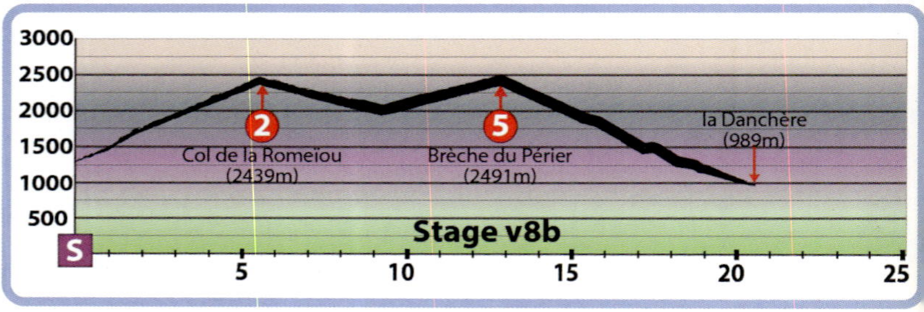

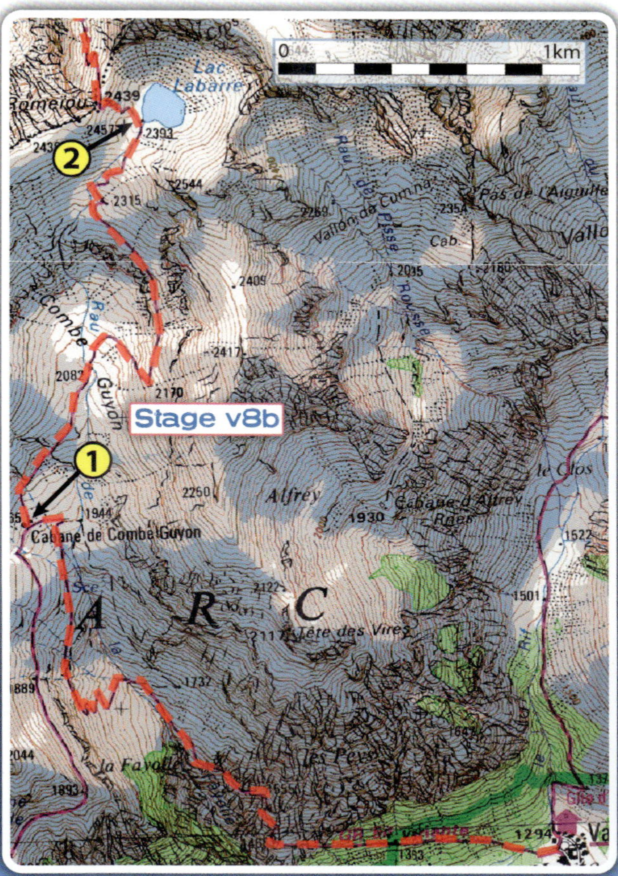

The ridge above Lac Labarre

v8b

S Head W from a signpost just below the gîte in **Valsenestre** ('Lac Labarre'). The path crosses a section of scree and then climbs across rocky slopes

1. 1:30: Arrive at **Cabane de Combe Guyon (1965m)**. Take the path on the right above the cabin and head N up the base of **Combe Guyon**. Cross the stream at the base of the combe and then bear right to climb the E flank of the combe. Soon the path bends left and heads N through rocky outcrops.

2. 3:00: Arrive at **Lac Labarre (2393m)**. Zigzag up to the NW to reach the nearby **Col de la Romeïou (2439m)**. Cross the col and descend on a path which snakes down across the slopes to the N. Watch your footing as the path is narrow and the drops are sheer.

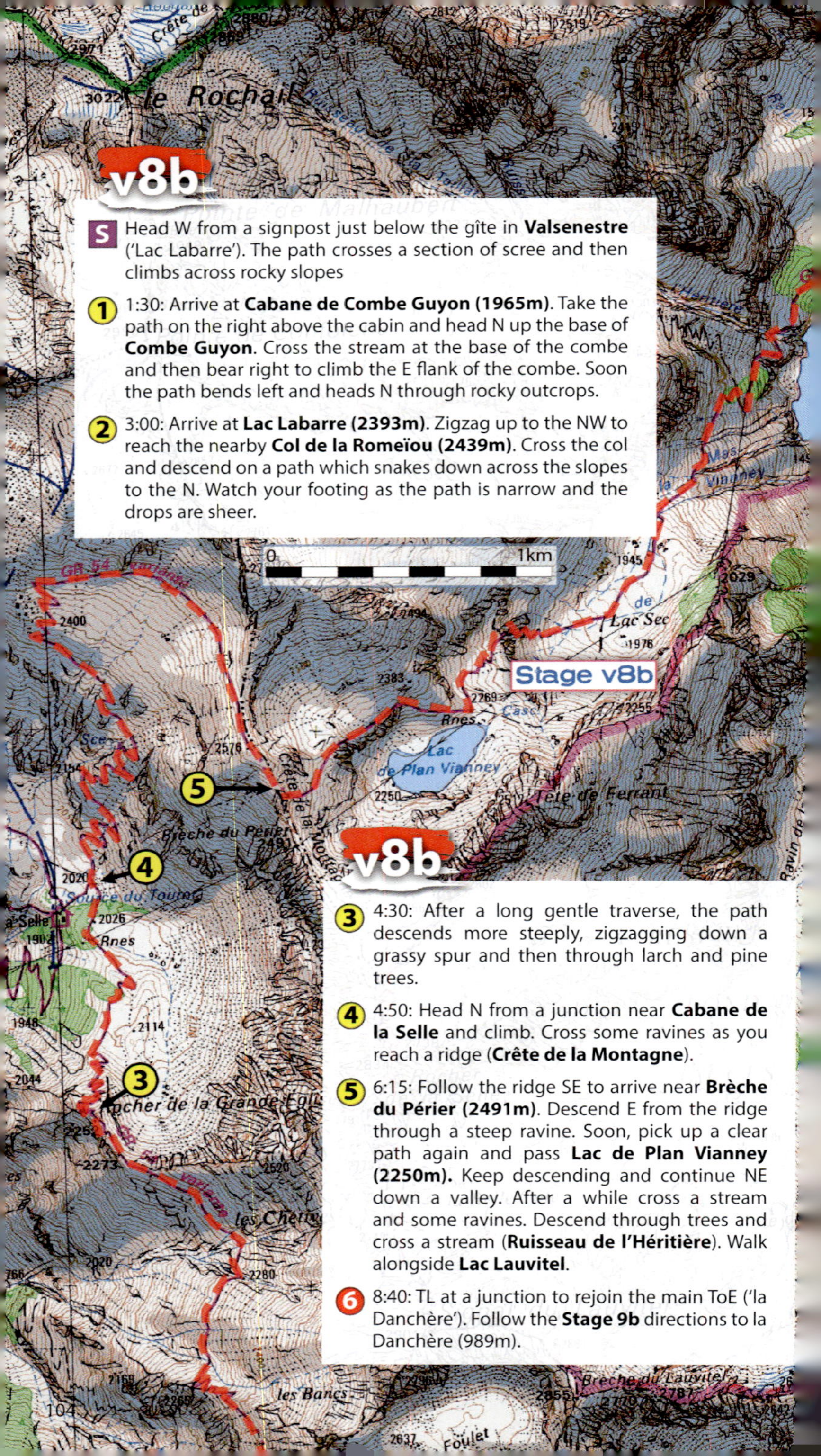

v8b

3. 4:30: After a long gentle traverse, the path descends more steeply, zigzagging down a grassy spur and then through larch and pine trees.

4. 4:50: Head N from a junction near **Cabane de la Selle** and climb. Cross some ravines as you reach a ridge (**Crête de la Montagne**).

5. 6:15: Follow the ridge SE to arrive near **Brèche du Périer (2491m)**. Descend E from the ridge through a steep ravine. Soon, pick up a clear path again and pass **Lac de Plan Vianney (2250m).** Keep descending and continue NE down a valley. After a while cross a stream and some ravines. Descend through trees and cross a stream (**Ruisseau de l'Héritière**). Walk alongside **Lac Lauvitel**.

6. 8:40: TL at a junction to rejoin the main ToE ('la Danchère'). Follow the **Stage 9b** directions to la Danchère (989m).

8b

S From **Valsenestre**, retrace your steps up the **Béranger valley**.

1. 0:30: TL at the junction passed on Stage 8a ('Col de la Muzelle'). Leave the track for a path on the left (yellow waymark). The path climbs beside of a rocky river bed (hard to follow; cairns). After a few minutes, cross the stream bed and climb on the other side.
2. 1:55: The path becomes faint across scree (cairns).
3. 2:15: The gradient increases significantly as the path climbs a very steep and exposed shale slope.
4. 3:00: Cross **Col de la Muzelle (2613m)** and descend steeply on a path (cairns).
5. 3:30: Head down the crest of a rocky spur. At the bottom of the spur, the path is faint (cairns). Cross a section of boulders. Just afterwards, TL and cross a stream. The path now descends the valley's W flank.
6. 3:45: Cross more boulders (cairns) and then rejoin the path. Soon, head along the W side of Lac de la Muzelle.
7. 4:15: Arrive at **Refuge de la Muzelle (2130m)**.

9a Refuge de la Muzelle to la Danchère

A trekker approaches Col du Vallon

There is a short climb through pastures to the final col of the ToE, the stunning Col du Vallon: there are superlative vistas of la Meije (3983m) and le Râteau (3809m). Then there is a long, relentless descent to Lac Lauvitel and its lovely reflections of the surrounding peaks. After a break to admire the views, continue descending all the way to the junction beside the hamlet of la Danchère: a short diversion off route takes you there.

Snow can lie near the col into July and occasionally, new snow can fall during summer. Even a light dusting of snow can make the paths near the col difficult to follow. Before Lac Lauvitel there are sections of slippery rocks to be scrambled down: the drops are steep so take care. On a few particularly tricky sections there are fixed cables. The descent after Lac Lauvitel is also rocky and slippery in the wet.

Time (hr:min)	4:30
Distance (km)	9.5
Ascent (m)	465
Descent (m)	1594
Max. altitude (m)	2531
Refreshments	la Danchère
Accommodation	Gîte at la Danchère

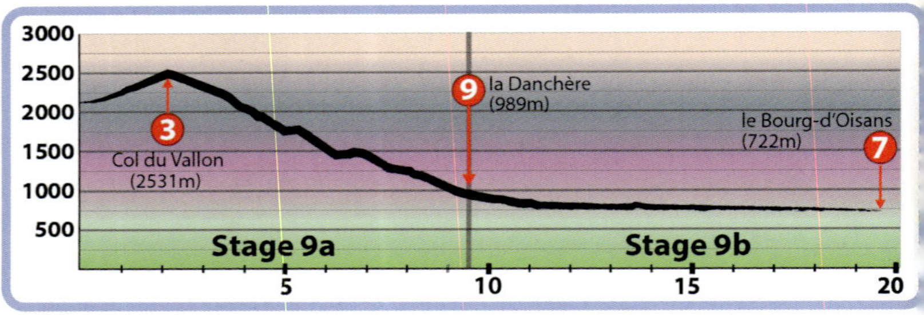

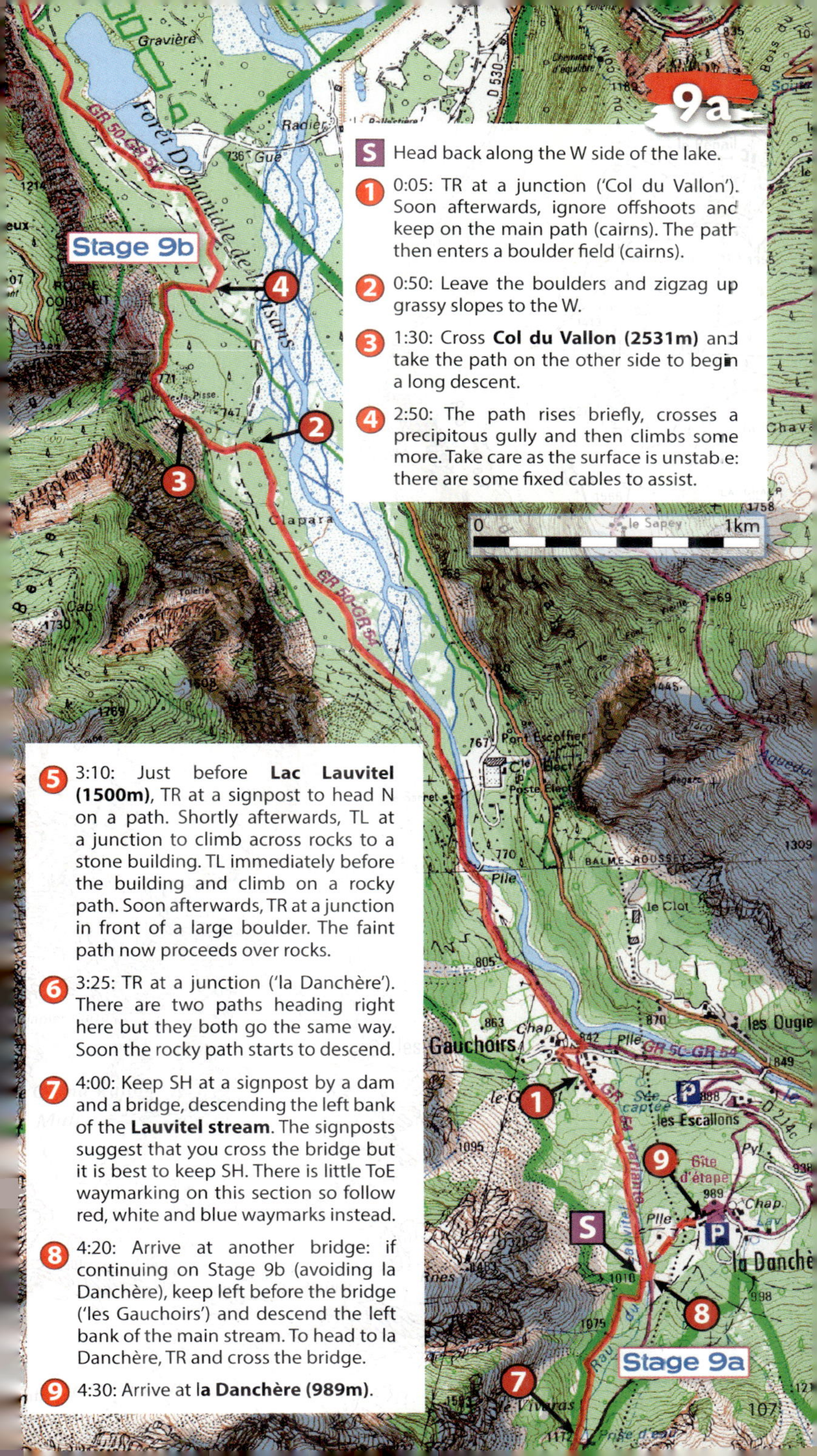

S Head back along the W side of the lake.

1 0:05: TR at a junction ('Col du Vallon'). Soon afterwards, ignore offshoots and keep on the main path (cairns). The path then enters a boulder field (cairns).

2 0:50: Leave the boulders and zigzag up grassy slopes to the W.

3 1:30: Cross **Col du Vallon (2531m)** and take the path on the other side to begin a long descent.

4 2:50: The path rises briefly, crosses a precipitous gully and then climbs some more. Take care as the surface is unstable: there are some fixed cables to assist.

5 3:10: Just before **Lac Lauvitel (1500m)**, TR at a signpost to head N on a path. Shortly afterwards, TL at a junction to climb across rocks to a stone building. TL immediately before the building and climb on a rocky path. Soon afterwards, TR at a junction in front of a large boulder. The faint path now proceeds over rocks.

6 3:25: TR at a junction ('la Danchère'). There are two paths heading right here but they both go the same way. Soon the rocky path starts to descend.

7 4:00: Keep SH at a signpost by a dam and a bridge, descending the left bank of the **Lauvitel stream**. The signposts suggest that you cross the bridge but it is best to keep SH. There is little ToE waymarking on this section so follow red, white and blue waymarks instead.

8 4:20: Arrive at another bridge: if continuing on Stage 9b (avoiding la Danchère), keep left before the bridge ('les Gauchoirs') and descend the left bank of the main stream. To head to la Danchère, TR and cross the bridge.

9 4:30: Arrive at **la Danchère (989m)**.

9b La Danchère to le Bourg d'Oisans

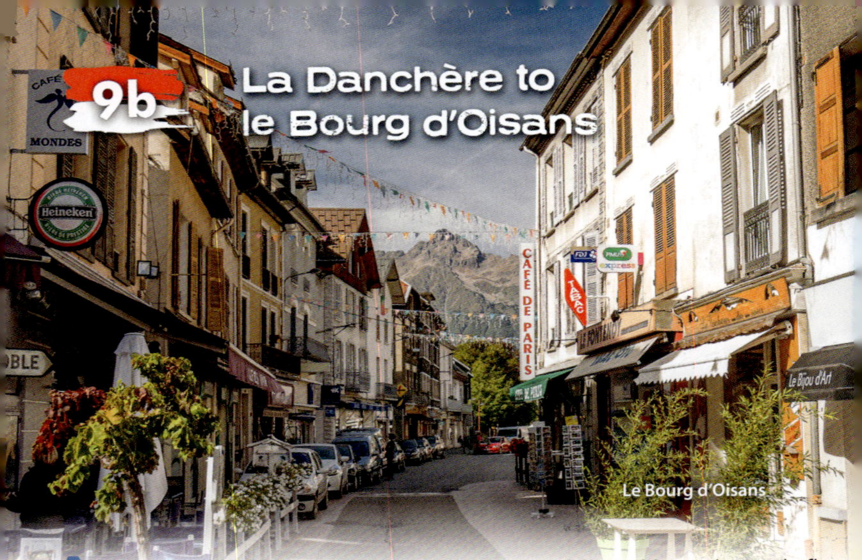

Le Bourg d'Oisans

A short descent via the village of les Gauchoirs is followed by a pleasantly flat valley walk to le Bourg d'Oisans. After completing the ToE, a well-deserved drink or meal awaits!

S Head back to the bridge crossed on Stage 9a. Cross it and TR ('les Gauchoirs') to descend the left bank of the main stream. Shortly afterwards, ignore another bridge. Immediately afterwards, keep right at a fork.

1 0:25: Keep SH and walk down the road through the village of **les Gauchoirs (852m)**. TR at a T-junction. Immediately afterwards, follow the road around to the right. Shortly afterwards, TL down a lane. After a few metres, TL at a signpost onto a gravel lane ('le Bourg-d'Oisans'). After a while, keep right at a fork by signpost.

2 1:10: TL at a junction.

3 1:15: Cross a footbridge and shortly afterwards, a waterfall (**Cascade de la Pisse**) comes into view.

4 1:25: TL at a junction onto another wide track, heading initially NE (waymark on tree). Ignore the path on the left at this junction. After 5min, keep SH at a junction still on the track. A few minutes later, keep SH at another junction. Keep SH at a wide junction with a barrier (signposted 'le Bourg-d'Oisans').

Time (hr:min)	2:30
Distance (km)	10.1
Ascent (m)	15
Descent (m)	281
Max. altitude (m)	988
Refreshments	Le Bourg d'Oisans
Accommodation	Le Vert & le Bourg d'Oisans

5 1:55: Keep SH at a junction (signposted 'le Bourg-d'Oisans'). The path soon arrives alongside the left bank of a river. Keep SH onto a road ('le Bourg-d'Oisans').

6 2:00: After a few minutes, at the entrance to the hamlet of **le Vert**, leave the road for a track on the left. After 5min, keep SH along a road.

7 2:25: Keep SH at a road junction. Continue SH along **Rue Humbert** to enter **le Bourg d'Oisans (722m)**. Then keep SH across a junction and walk down **Rue Docteur Daday**. After a few minutes, TR onto **Rue de Viennois**.

F 2:30: Continue SH until the junction with **Rue de Docteur Faure**: the tourist office is diagonally to the left.

Lac Lauvitel (Stage 9a)

Parc national des Ecrins

National Park Rules

A National Park is a unique landscape, open to everyone, and is everyone's responsibility. The park is protected by the application of rules. Thank you for respecting them.

No dogs, even on a lead.

Do not pick or remove anything.

No weapons allowed.

Do not leave any litter.

No fires allowed.

Do not make noise or disturb the wildlife.

No camping allowed.

Bivouac permitted up to one hour's walk from the park boundaries between 7pm and 9am.

Traffic is regulated

Toute infraction peut donner lieu à une amende. (Complément sur Décret N° 2009-448 du 21 avril 2009).

No mountain biking allowed.

Fishing prohibited in some lakes.

Drones and model aircraft prohibited.

Balisage des limites du cœur du Parc national des Écrins.